CONVERSATIONS

AFRICAN AND AFRICAN AMERICAN ARTWORKS IN DIALOGUE

FROM THE COLLECTIONS OF THE SMITHSONIAN NATIONAL MUSEUM
OF AFRICAN ART AND CAMILLE O. AND WILLIAM H. COSBY JR.

C O N V E R

EDITED BY

Christine Mullen Kreamer and Adrienne L. Childs

WITH ADDITIONAL CONTRIBUTIONS BY

Camille O. Cosby, William H. Cosby Jr., and David C. Driskell

With the assistance of Bryna Freyer, René Hanks, and Katharine E. Monsted

Smithsonian
National Museum of African Art

WASHINGTON, D.C.

SATIONS

AFRICAN AND AFRICAN AMERICAN ARTWORKS IN DIALOGUE

FROM THE COLLECTIONS OF THE SMITHSONIAN NATIONAL MUSEUM OF AFRICAN ART AND CAMILLE O. AND WILLIAM H. COSBY JR.

Conversations: African and African American Artworks in Dialogue from the Collections of the Smithsonian National Museum of African Art and Camille O. and William H. Cosby Jr. is published in conjunction with the exhibition of the same name, organized by and on view at the National Museum of African Art, Smithsonian Institution, Washington, D.C., November 9, 2014–January 24, 2016.

Conversations: African and African American Artworks in Dialogue
© 2014 National Museum of African Art, Smithsonian Institution

Library of Congress Control Number: 2014950901
ISBN 978-0-9656001-4-9

Published in 2014 by the National Museum of African Art, Smithsonian Institution

Visit the museum at 950 Independence Avenue, SW, Washington, D.C., and find us online at africa.si.edu.

MIGS GROVE, MANAGING EDITOR
JANE BOBKO, MANUSCRIPT EDITOR
LISA BUCK VANN, DESIGNER

PRINTED IN ICELAND BY ODDI PRINTING

PHOTOGRAPHY CREDITS

Franko Khoury: all artworks from the collection of the Smithsonian National Museum of African Art

Frank Stewart: figs. 2–4, 16, 17, 27, 28, 31, 32, 40, 45–47, 56, 61, 67–70, 78, 96, 102; pls. 5–7, 9, 10, 28, 36, 37, 47–49, 51, 52, 66, 69, 115–17, 121; cover inside flap, half title page; © Romare Bearden Foundation/Licensed by VAGA, New York: figs. 5, 90, 104, pl. 98, 99, 146; Estate of Norman W. Lewis, courtesy landor Fine Arts, New Jersey: fig. 10; courtesy Samella Lewis: fig. 13, pl. 8; courtesy the artists: figs. 14, 33, 43, 71, 73, 79, 82, 83, 88, pls. 11, 31, 53, 54, 68, 70, 71, 94, 95, 100, 147; Faith Ringgold © 1988: fig. 18, pl. 106; © Heirs of Aaron Douglas/Licensed by VAGA, New York: fig. 25, pl. 50; courtesy the Estate of Claude Clark: fig. 26; © Valerie Gerrard Browne, courtesy the Chicago History Museum: figs. 29, 60, 108, pls. 38, 141, 142; © 1971 The Charles White Archives: figs. 34, 48, pl. 33; © 1968 The Charles White Archives: figs. 35, 58, pl. 32; © Catlett Mora Family Trust/Licensed by VAGA, New York: figs. 36, 59, pls. 13, 34, 35, front cover left, title page right; © 2014 The Jacob and Gwendolyn Lawrence Foundation, Seattle/Artists Rights Society (ARS), New York: figs. 37, 109, pls. 143, 144; © Estate of Bob Thompson, courtesy Michael Rosenfeld Gallery LLC, New York: figs. 38, 39, 100, pl. 118; Estate of Charles Alston: fig. 41, pl. 30; courtesy Charles Thomas Lewis: fig. 42, pl. 120; Loïs Mailou Jones Pierre-Noel Trust: fig. 89, pl. 96; © Estate of Hughie Lee-Smith/Licensed by VAGA, New York: fig. 101, pl. 119; Estate of Beauford Delaney, by permission of Derek L. Spratley, Esq., court-appointed administrator: fig. 110, pl. 145; courtesy the Hayden Family Revocable Art Trust: pl. 67; © Varnette P. Honeywood, 1984, permission granted by Varnette P. Honeywood Estate: pl. 97

Becket Logan: figs. 8, 57, pl. 29

Smithsonian Institution: figs. 21–23

David Stansbury: © Benton Testamentary Trusts/UMB Bank Trustee/VAGA, New York: fig. 11; © 1968 The Charles White Archives: fig. 12

Jerry Thompson: figs. 93, 94, pls. 104, 107; courtesy the artists: figs. 15, 95, pl. 101, 105; © Estate of Jean-Michel Basquiat/ADAGP, Paris/ARS, New York 2014: pl. 12; courtesy The Hanks Family: pl. 102; courtesy Catherine Hanks: pl. 103

Glenn Virgin: courtesy the artist: figs. 20, 30

Gene Young: courtesy Smithsonian American Art Museum: fig. 24

HALF TITLE PAGE

James Lesesne Wells
Georgetown Garden (detail)
plate 10

TITLE PAGE, LEFT

Kongo artist, Angola, Democratic Republic of the Congo, Republic of the Congo
Female figure with child *(niongi)* (detail)
plate 2

TITLE PAGE, RIGHT

Elizabeth Catlett
Maternity (detail)
plate 13

Contents

Foreword

—Asante *adrinka* symbol

Go back to fetch it.
—Asante proverb, Ghana

You can't know where
you are going if you
don't know where you
have been.
—African American saying

THE ASANTE ADINKRA SYMBOL *sankofa,* which depicts a bird looking backward to preen itself, cues the Asante proverb, which resonates with the African American saying. Both maxims are appropriate for *Conversations: African and African American Artworks in Dialogue* and communicate the same message: learn from your experience, don't forget your past, respect ancestral tradition. This exhibition and publication celebrate the fiftieth anniversary of the Smithsonian National Museum of African Art, recognizing the museum's unique history and its enduring role in using the power of art to "wake somebody up," as the African American artist Elizabeth Catlett so often said and affirmed

vii

through her work. They bring together major works of art from two world-class collections—the National Museum of African Art and the collection of Camille O. and William H. Cosby Jr. The Cosbys' decision to share African American artworks from their collection with the public for the very first time—with the exception of the loan of one work of art—is extraordinarily generous. It reflects their understanding of the importance of the National Museum of African Art and its central place in fostering meaningful dialogue about ideas and issues that unite us all.

Conversations acknowledges the visionary leadership of Warren M. Robbins, a retired Foreign Service officer who founded the private Museum of African Art on Capitol Hill, in Washington, D.C., in 1964. As Asif Shaikh, a valued member of our advisory board, eloquently stated, "Warren saw the opportunity to use art to help bridge America's greatest divide—the gap between black and white." Robbins created "a space for what unites rather than what divides." [1]

The Museum of African Art, opened during the challenging times of the civil rights movement, centered its efforts on education in, and dialogue about, the arts. This strategy, Robbins felt, would address the appalling state of race relations that persisted in the United States at that time. Located in a townhouse on A Street NE that had been the home of Frederick Douglass, the museum was a place where works of both African and African American art were collected and displayed. In 1979, when the museum became part of the Smithsonian Institution, its collecting mission was redefined to focus exclusively on the arts of Africa, resulting in the transfer of many of its African American artworks to the Smithsonian American Art Museum, where they remain today.

Since the opening of the Smithsonian National Museum of African Art on the National Mall in 1987, the museum has expanded its collection of outstanding works of African art, but it has also continued, through exhibitions and programs, to emphasize

fig. 1 | OVERLEAF

[plate 57]
Ousmane Sow
born 1935, Senegal
Toussaint Louverture et la vieille esclave (Toussaint Louverture and the Elderly Slave) (detail)
1989
Mixed media (iron, earth, jute, straw)
220 x 100 x 110 cm
(86 5/8 x 39 3/8 x 43 5/16 in.)
National Museum of African Art, Smithsonian Institution, museum purchase, through exchange from Emil Eisenberg, and Mr. and Mrs. Norman Robbins, and with funds from Stuart Bohart and Barbara Portman, 2009-8-1

connections between Africa and the African diaspora. Thus *Conversations* looks both to the museum's past and to its future in demonstrating the relevance of Africa and Africa's arts to succeeding generations the world over.

How I look at connections between African and African American art reflects some of my personal history—or, shall I say, herstory. I grew up in Jacksonville, Florida, in the days of legalized segregation. There were no art galleries or museums in my hometown that welcomed me or any other African American. But, I was fortunate to grow up in a home adorned with framed works of art and small sculptures.

On the coffee table were books that, as a four- and five-year-old girl, I would kneel in front of and turn page after page to savor the images. Visits to the home of my great-grandfather, A. L. Lewis, invariably found me entranced with a mahogany letter opener made in Africa and with a photograph of my great-grandfather and his wife, Elzona Lewis, as they sat on camels in front of pyramids in Egypt in 1935. Such distinctive memories about people, places, and objects reinforced how, even as a youngster, I saw African and African American art in whole, not broken, terms, and how I saw positive connections between the peoples of Africa and the African diaspora.

Today, as the director of the Smithsonian National Museum of African Art, I have the opportunity to witness visual conversations between African and African American artists, to consider ways in which African American art has been and continues to be in dialogue with African art, and to observe nuanced and inspiring connections between African and African American artists. These connections greet us from a place of power and strength, from a place of wholeness.

Every exhibition and book project at the National Museum of African Art relies upon the contributions of many individuals. First and foremost, I would like to express my deepest gratitude to Drs. Bill and Camille Cosby for sharing their collection with our

museum and our visitors. I would also like to thank the team of four exceptional curators who worked together to realize *Conversations:* David C. Driskell, artist, scholar, and
curator of the Cosby collection, and Adrienne L. Childs, independent scholar, who are
both specialists in African American art; and, from our museum, Africanist art historians Bryna Freyer, curator, and Christine Mullen Kreamer, deputy director and chief
curator, who also provided outstanding leadership of the entire project.

This undertaking could not have been realized without the assistance of René
Hanks, who was particularly helpful in facilitating access to and information about
works of art in the Cosby collection. Sondra Pugh and Rodney Moore were invaluable
in providing logistical support to the curatorial team. MFM Design, under the creative
leadership of Richard Molinaroli, is to be commended for the exhibition's elegant and
engaging design. Jerry Thompson and Glenn Virgin graciously responded to our requests
for new photography of selected works of art. I am also appreciative of the work of our
manuscript editor for this project, Jane Bobko.

I would like to applaud the museum's exceptional staff, for each brings singular
expertise to the realization of our exhibitions, publications, programs, and outreach.
I am grateful for their professionalism and commitment to their work. For this project
in particular, I wish to acknowledge Migs Grove for her management of the editorial
process, Kate Monsted for her assistance in every phase of the work, and Lisa Vann
for her stunning design of this publication and the exhibition graphics. Colleen Foran
provided editorial assistance, and Jeremy Jelenfy assisted with the publication images
and produced the exhibition graphics. Steve Mellor and Clarissa Fostel brought their
considerable professionalism and expertise to bear in the assessment, crating, and
shipping of the Cosby collection to our museum. Douglas Johnston worked closely with
MFM as he managed exhibition construction. Amy Staples oversaw the processing of

museum images for this publication. She was ably assisted by Sara Manco, Nathan Sowry, and Jessica Suworoff. Franko Khoury spent many hours photographing the works of African art illustrated in this volume. Research conducted by intern Jalene Regassa informed the project's thematic organization. Aaron Ballew graciously provided outstanding audiovisual technical assistance at a critical moment. Bonnie Berry and Bill Holmes provided invaluable administrative assistance throughout.

A fiftieth anniversary offers the opportunity to reflect upon a half century of history and to look forward to the next half century. Looking back, we recognize our founder, Warren M. Robbins, the directors who succeeded him—Sylvia H. Williams, Roslyn Adele Walker, and Sharon F. Patton—and the commitment to arts education and outreach that has remained at the heart of our museum's mission all these years. Looking forward, we chart an ambitious course for our future, confident that Africa's arts and global relevance will continue to resonate with an ever-increasing number of visitors from around the world. As I consider the intersecting themes explored in *Conversations: African and African American Artworks in Dialogue,* and the magnificent works of art featured in the exhibition and this publication, I am truly amazed, humbled, and grateful for the power of art to move us deeply and to bring us an awareness of our shared stories and our common humanity. Let the conversations continue. Onward!

—Johnnetta Betsch Cole
Director, National Museum of African Art

NOTE

1. Asif Shaikh, remarks at a reception held at the Smithsonian National Museum of African Art, Washington, D.C., January 16, 2014. For more on the history of the museum, see Binkley et al. 2011.

Preface

THROUGHOUT THE AGES, art has been relied upon to unite peoples of the world in different places and to help bring about cultural understanding and define common grounds of interest. This exhibition, comprised of selected works from the collections of a leading public museum and a private family, explores visual and intellectual common ground in artworks made by African and African American artists. It celebrates the National Museum of African Art's fiftieth anniversary and recognizes the museum's early history when, as a private museum on Capitol Hill, the Museum of African Art sought to build bridges of cross-cultural understanding through collecting and exhibiting both African and African American art. In *Conversations: African and African American Artworks in Dialogue,* over a hundred works by African artists from the collection of the National Museum of African Art are exhibited alongside more than sixty works by African American artists from the collection of Drs. Camille O. and William H. Cosby Jr. Never before has an exhibition been assembled comprising works of art from the Cosby collection; Henry Ossawa Tanner's *The Thankful Poor* (SEE FIG. 67, PLATE 47) is the only painting that has been loaned prior to this historic showing.[1] This important collaboration between one of the nation's prized museums and a private collection will, one hopes, become a model for future exhibitions in the new millennium.

There are a number of reasons why African American art should rightly be seen in the company of African art. The most notable is the heritage that many African American artists acknowledge. In previous publications and interviews I have noted the recent rise of scholarly interest in the subject of Africa and its diaspora in the Americas. At the forefront of this discussion is the role that art plays in connecting African American visual culture to numerous and varied cultural expressions in West and central Africa, a subject of study that is more than a century old. Yet very few exhibitions over the past century have attempted to bring together major works by African and African American artists.

The convergences of and parallels between Africa's arts and those created by African American artists are not always easily observed. For example, one could ask why African American artists evinced no interest in acknowledging an ancestral relationship with the arts of Africa until the late nineteenth and early twentieth centuries. A close review of African American history, however, will explain the lack of what the art historian Robert Farris Thompson calls "African retentions"[2] in the visual culture of African American artists in the United States before the late nineteenth century. First, for those subjugated by slavery it was not practical to create works of art that celebrated their own interest in self-definition and freedom of expression. Second, the changes that occurred in the lifestyles of people of African ancestry in America had to fit within the governing beliefs of a slave society that was based on Eurocentric principles. It was for these reasons that much of the artistry practiced by African Americans prior to the end of the period of slavery in the United States was quietly disguised among utilitarian and service-oriented objects and practices. African American artists found little or no use in making African-inspired ceremonial objects in a society where such religious practices and their material forms were forbidden. Although a few examples of African artistic practice survived in selected architectural and crafts traditions, they were primarily functional forms connected to everyday use. In pottery and textiles, and particularly in quilt making, the creation of an aesthetic statement that was African-based was more evident, but even here overt connections to Africa were disguised or encoded in secret symbols or hidden information.

African American artists such as Robert S. Duncanson and Edward Mitchell Bannister began the study of painting prior to emancipation, but few works by them address the subject of slavery and the cruel conditions under which black people had lived for more than two centuries. The goal that black artists most often pursued was to demonstrate an artistry and professionalism equal (or superior) to those of their white contemporaries. For example, Duncanson exhibits a mastery of the European literary landscape in *Vale of Kashmir* (FIG. 2, PLATE 6). In this work he captures the mood of a mythical landscape, yet indirectly he suggests a desire for harmony among the races as befits the idyllic scene his painting depicts. There are subtle exceptions where race-consciousness fleetingly emerges. While Joshua Johnston, whose work predates both Duncanson's and Bannister's, devoted much of his time to painting portraits of people of class and distinction, mainly wealthy white people of Baltimore, there are several portraits of African Americans that have been attributed to his hand, though none of them are to be found in the Cosby collection of African American art. Mary Edmonia Lewis's mixed racial heritage (First Nations and African American) does manifest itself in a scene such as *Marriage of Hiawatha* (PLATE 116), a sculpture executed in the neoclassical tradition.

African American artists who traveled to Europe to study in the first quarter of the twentieth century, particularly those who chose to work in Paris, became increasingly aware of the high regard in which European modernists held traditional African art. As early as 1906 the American photographer Robert Small recorded scenes in Pablo Picasso's Parisian studio in which numerous examples of West African art adorn the walls. Many European artists generated interest as they used various African masks and statuary as inspiring sources in their work. It was the original intention of the Museum of African Art's founder, Warren M. Robbins, to demonstrate that European modernism was heavily indebted to African art. He had emphasized this point when he displayed a small collection of modern European art from his own collection in 1962 at the Howard University Gallery of Art, and he pressed the matter again in the Museum of African Art's comparative gallery. Robbins knew that several African American artists had looked to African art as informing sources for their work in the 1920s, but he was initially unaware of the interest that some artists expressed as early as the turn of the twentieth century. Meta Vaux Warrick Fuller, whose work *Peace Halting the Ruthlessness of War* (FIG. 4, PLATE 66) is included in *Conversations,* was among the first African American artists to incorporate in her work the iconography of Egyptian art. (Since the early decades of the twentieth century in particular, many African Americans have viewed the art of ancient Egypt as one of the major achievements of African culture.)

In the 1920s, African American artists began to look seriously at African art

fig. 4
[plate 66]
Meta Vaux Warrick Fuller
1877–1968, United States
Peace Halting the Ruthlessness of War
1917, cast 1998
Bronze
35.5 x 42.5 x 22.9 cm
(14 x 16 3/4 x 9 in.)
The Collection of Camille O. and William H. Cosby Jr.

and to use it as a source of inspiration in their work; the philosopher Alain LeRoy Locke
was the most vocal advocate of that perspective. The affirmation of this trust was evident in the coalescing of a black cultural movement within the burgeoning arts community in New York's Harlem neighborhood. The concerted consciousness-raising effort on
the part of Locke, W. E. B. Du Bois, and others brought arts and letters into the service of
progress, cultural edification, and political advancement, and gave rise to the New
Negro movement and, later, to what is now known as the Harlem Renaissance.

Conversations is not designed to review or reestablish the governing principles by
which the Harlem Renaissance defined itself or to suggest a one-to-one correspondence
between African and African American art. Instead, this juxtaposition of African art with
the art created by African American artists over the past two centuries explores con-
verging ideas, intersecting themes, and parallel likenesses found in the works of African
and diasporic artists across a broad spectrum of time and space. To be sure, historical
patterns of control and oppression observed in both African American and African social
and cultural contexts have had divergent influences on visual expressions. For instance,
the works created by African artists who lived under colonial subjection in places such
as the Congo, Ghana, Nigeria, and Sierra Leone adhered to traditional forms of art making that related to service and function in their own societies. Conversely, the art that
was made by African Americans in the period of slavery, Jim Crow, and segregation of
the races did not, in the main, serve the black community as a vessel of tradition. Instead,
during a time when racism was an accepted and sanctioned institution in all walks of life,
some African American artists felt it was necessary to prove themselves highly capable of
rendering and presenting to the American public works of art that aided their own cultural emancipation from the confines of blackness in American society.

When considering the collection of Camille and Bill Cosby, a collection comprising

principally works by African American artists, one should be
aware that the works were not assembled in a chronological
manner. My role as curator of the collection was to ascertain
the Cosbys' interest in both older and more contemporary art
by African American artists. It should be noted that the Cosbys
had already collected a broad spectrum of American art, including works by Thomas Hart Benton, Stuart Davis, George Inness,
Reginald Marsh, and Georgia O'Keefe, among others. Their
catholic taste in collecting was an assurance to me that they
had decided to acquire important artworks by American masters
prior to the time that I began advising them, in 1978. I knew my
role to be one of adding works of significant quality to those
already obtained, with particular emphasis on works by African
American artists. Importantly, by having recently curated several
exhibitions that emphasized the establishment of a quality
canon in African American art, I was keenly aware of works of art
that were on the market at that time. Although it was necessary
to collect artworks that were readily available, both Bill and
Camille Cosby made inquiries of me from time to time about the
availability of works that they had seen in various exhibitions,
including some works that were housed at historically black colleges and universities.

   During the entire period of my assembling major works for the collection, such as
Tanner's *The Thankful Poor* (SEE FIG. 67, PLATE 47), Bill kept alive his sense of humor about
why the Cosbys felt the need to collect African American art. On one occasion he re-
minded me that I could not buy for them what I desired to see them own. Why? His

fig. 5 | LEFT, TOP

[plate 99]
Romare Bearden
1911–1988, United States
Harlem Brownstone
1980
Collage on Masonite
75.8 x 101.5 cm
(29 7/8 x 40 in.)
The Collection of Camille O.
and William H. Cosby Jr.

fig. 6 | LEFT, BELOW

[plate 81]
Zwelethu Mthethwa
born 1960, South Africa
Untitled
2002
Chromogenic print mounted
on Plexiglas
96.5 x 129.5 cm (38 x 51 in.)
National Museum of African
Art, Smithsonian Institution,
museum purchase, 2003-11-1

fig. 7

[plate 43]
Kongo artist, Democratic
Republic of the Congo,
Republic of the Congo
Crucifix
17th century
Copper alloy
21.6 x 17.5 x 3.5 cm
(8 1/2 x 6 7/8 x 1 3/8 in.)
National Museum of African
Art, Smithsonian Institution,
gift of Walt Disney World
Co., a subsidiary of The Walt
Disney Company, 2005-6-106

response was, "Because it is not your money." After Camille presented Bill with *The Thankful Poor* as a Christmas gift in December 1981, he phoned me to ask, "What about the companion piece, *The Banjo Lesson*?" I responded by saying, "It is in the collection of Hampton University, and it is not for sale." Bill's humorous retort was, "Well, how much is Hampton?" Working in a pleasant environment, while at the same time being challenged to obtain the very finest African American works available, became the nexus of an enduring friendship and an engaging practice combining respect and a creative outlook on collecting.

Romare Bearden's *Harlem Brownstone* (FIGS. 5, 90, PLATE 99) seems to welcome the presence of a handsomely crafted chromogenic print by the South African artist Zwelethu Mthethwa (FIG. 6, PLATE 81) with the same ease that Aaron Douglas's *Crucifixion* (SEE FIG. 25, PLATE 50) enters into a dialogue with a crucifix by an anonymous seventeenth-century Congolese artist (FIG. 7, PLATE 43). In imagining the beauty and composure of black women, the African American artist William Henry Johnson (FIGS. 8, 57, PLATE 29) and the Senegalese artist M'boz Faye (FIG. 9, PLATE 24) appear to work in tandem as they illuminate the quiet mystery of the female figure. Over the past century, African American men and women have made quilts whose patterns and thematic content invite comparison with certain textiles and tapestries made by traditional African artists. Such similarities in iconography over centuries approach a shared, timeless understanding of the language of form.

Conversations continues an important dialogue linking African and African diasporan history and expressive culture, and it is by no means the last word. The exhibition opens the door to an often neglected conversation within the African diaspora about the cultural connections that enhance the common practice of art making in Africa and America. The works by African and African American artists presented in this exhibition and publication reach across time and space, and share many forms, themes, and sensibilities, thus giving credence to the notion that all art emanates from a common desire to communicate the diverse expressions of the human experience.

—David C. Driskell

NOTES

1. *The Thankful Poor* was shown in 1987 at the Pennsylvania Academy of the Fine Arts, Philadelphia, as part of the exhibition *Hidden Heritage: Afro-American Art, 1800–1950,* which I curated. The painting was not shown in other venues of the exhibition, which began at the Bellevue Art Museum, Washington, in 1985 and traveled until 1988.

2. See R. Thompson 1984.

fig. 8 | OPPOSITE

[plate 29]
William Henry Johnson
1901–1970, United States
Untitled (Seated Woman)
1939
Tempera and gouache on
paper
61 x 45.8 cm (24 x 18 in.)
The Collection of Camille O.
and William H. Cosby Jr.

fig. 9 | RIGHT

[plate 24]
M'boz Faye
n.d., Senegal
Untitled
1970
Paint on burlap
66.8 x 56.9 x 4.4 cm
(26 5/16 x 22 3/8 x 1 3/4 in.)
National Museum of African
Art, Smithsonian Institution,
gift of Samella Lewis,
2010-14-18

Collecting Priorities: A Conversation with Bill and Camille Cosby

David C. Driskell, with Adrienne L. Childs and Christine Mullen Kreamer

N DECEMBER 13, 2013, Bill and Camille Cosby sat down with the curators David C. Driskell, Adrienne L. Childs, and Christine Mullen Kreamer to discuss the Cosbys' journey as collectors, their passion for art by African American artists, and their reasons for sharing their extraordinary collection with the world for the first time.

DAVID C. DRISKELL | What are your earliest recollections of art?

BILL COSBY | I think it's important to explain that I was born into a family of low economic status. The home that I remember was on Stewart Street in Philadelphia. It had just cold water, and the toilet was outside. The only art I remember seeing was in a book with pictures that my mother read to my brother James and me when we were young. That was the only art that I recall existing in this house in North Philadelphia—we never toured the museum.

We then moved to a new, wonderful housing project called the Richard Allen projects, and everything was cement, brick, iron, glass—no wood at all. The only art that existed was in the form of furniture design, patterned linoleum, wooden items in the kitchen and the hallway. My father worked in a steel foundry where they made iron things, and he was able to make two beds. To this day I don't know where those beds are, but there were two beds with the same design—twin beds, because in those days, in the 1940s, people slept in twin beds. And then he brought home two other beds that had painted designs on them.

Then art came into our lives by way of *Jet* and *Ebony* magazines. We cut out pictures of celebrities from these magazines and hung them on our walls with some Scotch tape, even in the living room. There was no framing of anything. So I grew up with pictures of celebrities cut from the covers of *Jet* and *Ebony* magazines, hand-made furniture, and the designs on the linoleum rug and a carpet my mother bought that went up the stairs. That was the only art that I remember in our home. In the homes of other friends of mine, who were of similar economic status, there would be photographs, but we didn't have any photographs. I think because we didn't know who was going to be famous! *[laughter]*

In the housing projects there were two things I remember. There was a place called "the Center" where there was a ping-pong room, a library, and a daycare center; and there was a commissioned artwork above the check-in desk. I cannot remember the name of the artist, but the work showed Jackie Robinson stealing home base, a basketball player, and Jesse Owens, done in pastel chalk. Also, behind the center, near the basketball court, was a large cement sculpture showing four chil-

fig. 10 | OVERLEAF

Norman Lewis
1909–1979, United States
Untitled (Family Portrait)
c. 1936
Oil on burlap
66.8 x 91.5 cm
(26 1/4 x 36 in.)
The Collection of Camille O.
and William H. Cosby Jr.

dren with African features in profile, and underneath it said, "Lift every voice and sing." Much later, in the 1980s, when I heard they were going to tear down the housing project, I wanted to buy "Lift every voice and sing." Unfortunately, they broke it, and that history is gone.

DRISKELL | Camille, I'd like to ask you about your early experiences with art. Now I know from our conversations that you knew some of the people who associated with your family in Washington who really were pioneers in helping to bring about consciousness, cultural consciousness, of African American art in the city of Washington in the 1940s and the 1950s. That must have made an impression on you, even though you may not have been able to put it in place at that time.

CAMILLE COSBY | I didn't understand the importance at the time, but I will give you some historical context. The city I was born in, Washington, D.C., in 1944 was legally segregated, thanks to the Supreme Court decision *[Plessy v. Ferguson]* in 1896. Because it was racially segregated, my world was made up of African American culture and consisted of African Americans in all kinds of professions and jobs— mechanics, teachers, pharmacists. One good friend of my father's was Mr. [Frederick] Aden, whose brother was Alonzo Aden, who started the Barnett Aden Gallery in the early 1940s, sometime before I was born. Mr. Aden, my father's friend, would always speak about his brother, but of course, like Bill, I did not see any paintings on the walls in our home, although photographs of family members or friends were placed on tabletops. But there was nothing else. I don't remember anything removed from *Ebony* magazine, which was in our home. We knew about the Barnett Aden Gallery, though we never went there. It never resonated at that time how important it was that Mr. [Alonzo] Aden was a prominent collector of African American art and that he started the gallery with James V. Herring, who was the founder of the art department at Howard University. All of that history did not resonate with me as a child, but it did resonate with me as an adult, especially after Bill and I began to collect African American art.

DRISKELL | What motivated you to collect, and what did you collect in the early days?

BILL COSBY | I began in that $5,000 house in the Richard Allen housing project with no art, and I eventually found myself working as an entertainer and going to the offices of Caucasian executives, and I would see them with pictures and oil paintings of their family members and other white people. I said to myself, I've got to put these things in my home, because I'm just tired of looking at all these white people, and I want black people in my house.

Now, I had a problem, because in those days, with the civil rights movement, *Time* and *Life* magazines were defining what the powerful black artists were doing. And they were drawing angry black people or stereotypical images of the mother and child. So I went to the Brockman Gallery in Los Angeles, which sold art by black artists. I saw a painting—it was round and orange like a poppy. It just made me feel very calm. I think I paid about seventy dollars. And I took it home, and Camille didn't mind, so I put it on the wall.

Then I went back to the Brockman Gallery to find some pieces for a television series I was doing at the time. The character I played was Chet Kincaid, and whenever you see any Chet Kincaid stories, every piece, every painting on the set was either purchased or borrowed from the Brockman Gallery for the show. Even on location, if we rented a home owned by some Caucasian people, those artworks came out and works by black artists went up.

I only picked artworks that gave me a feeling of calm, because I couldn't stand to come home to the stereotypical images of mother and child or angry black people after dealing with some of the racist people I encountered during the day.

Thomas Hart Benton
1889–1975, United States
The Bible Lesson
c. 1940
Tempera on canvas mounted
on panel
83.8 x 101.5 cm (33 x 40 in.)
The Collection of Camille O.
and William H. Cosby Jr.

When I did *The Cosby Mysteries,* after the Huxtables [on *The Cosby Show*], I put a collection of the Blue Note LPs in the hallway of my character Guy Hanks's apartment, because Blue Note had African American men and women, jazz musicians, on 98 percent of the covers, and with the lettering and everything, that was art. Then we moved into Guy Hanks's living room and there's Eric Dolphy in a huge painting, copied from a photograph. And so every series with the name Cosby, if it had to do with a character who lived in a house, you'd better believe that the sets included works by artists who are represented by galleries that sell African American art.

Our collection began to grow and grow and grow, especially in the late 1960s after the television series *I Spy,* as we zoomed financially and began buying houses and needed art to fill them. However, we didn't have a David Driskell in those early days. We just had go-out-to-Brockman-and-come-back-with-something.

CAMILLE COSBY | We have collected works by artists who are *not* African American. We have representations of Thomas Hart Benton (FIG. 11), Reginald Marsh, George Inness, Maurice Prendergast. We have collected Shaker furniture, which can also be considered artistic. We do have other representations in our collection, but our main focus has been on African American art, because we are African American people with a lot of pride about our African American heritages.

My husband has been very important in terms of enlightening me about the significance of selecting anything that we have collected throughout the years. In January 2014 we celebrated our fiftieth wedding anniversary, and we have many things that we have collected together over the years, but we didn't collect anything for its monetary value. We only collect for the emotional value. Every single thing that we have is because we really love living with it, and that's the bottom line.

Because I grew up in a segregated environment, Charles White's portraits of black people are familiar to me. The colors that are in paintings and collages by

Romare Bearden and by Bob Thompson, and the colors that are in your paintings, David, are meaningful to me. I mean, colors were always important to African people, but some of that was lost when they were enslaved and they were forced to lose so many things. So colors have always been important to me. I know now, in retrospect, that some of the artworks in our collection are so important to me because they are familiar to me. When I was growing up, my father and mother would always take us on nature walks or on drives, so the landscapes of Robert S. Duncanson resonate with me because they remind me of the beauty I saw on these family excursions. Or even if you take a Norman Lewis, with the children seated with their father while he is reading a newspaper, that's familiar to me because that's my dad (FIG. 10). I remember him reading a paper all the time and we would sit with him. Or if you look at a work by Elizabeth Catlett, infused with her pride about being a woman, and her inner strength, those are the women who are familiar to me from my childhood (SEE PLATE 13; FIG. 59, PLATE 35).

The importance of family was very significant in the segregated community in which I grew up. We looked out for each other, cared for one another, showed respect for the elders and respect for children, which I think has dissipated a lot in our current history. All of that was so significant, and certainly formed me, but also helped me to make the selections that I eventually made in terms of our collection.

DRISKELL | Can you speak more about the appeal that works by Charles White hold for you?

CAMILLE COSBY | It was the Heritage Gallery in Los Angeles where I first encountered works by Charles White. I just fell in love with the people in his paintings, and his use of Chinese ink and charcoal was just fantastic. And even now, when I walk past those paintings, I try to understand the social commentary coming from them,

fig. 12 | OPPOSITE

Charles White
1918–1979, United States
Bill
1968
Charcoal on artist's board
144.8 x 84.5 cm
(57 x 33 1/4 in.)
The Collection of Camille O.
and William H. Cosby Jr.

because Charles had a message in each one of his paintings, that's for sure. But my favorite was the one he did of Bill (FIG. 12), because people perceived him as a funny performer, but Charles captured Bill's seriousness, the introspection. You know, peeling away the layers and getting to the bottom of human behavior is manifested in all of his work. My husband may laugh, but it's true, I've always loved that painting.

BILL COSBY | It was *Ebony* magazine that really introduced me to the work of Charles White, because, if you remember, *Ebony* magazine featured Charles White's artwork and Lerone Bennett Jr.'s writings. They had chosen Charles White to be their artist.

DRISKELL | I'm sure that one of the things you were looking at was his concept of images of dignity, because you wanted positive images of African Americans.

BILL COSBY | You know what it also was? In Charles White's portraits, whether you were a man or a woman, he would give you a pair of arms and hands that looked like they could lift a wagon. And, to me, that symbolically stands for our people in the South moving to the North to work, and working, lifting, pulling, washing, cleaning. In my own portrait, they don't look like my arms. In White's compositions of women in some of the paintings that we have, you will see serenity in the woman's face, and then her forearms really speak of that washtub, really speak of wringing those clothes out, really speak of lifting children, lifting things, fixing things, moving things (SEE FIGS. 35, 58, PLATE 32).

DRISKELL | Labor with dignity.

CAMILLE COSBY | I would like to say another thing about Charles White's images. I like the fact that his women did not reflect what has always been propagandized about feminine, female beauty. He went totally against that and just showed the strength and the tenacity of black women, and not at the expense of black males, but just their own strength to get through as black and female. He did not try to capitalize on the propaganda, which is still quite egregious.

DRISKELL | What about works in your collection by other artists?

BILL COSBY | I want to point out Richmond Barthé. When you look at a work by Richmond Barthé, you cannot help, with so many of his pieces, but see the body and the shape of his subjects. His prizefighter [*The Boxer,* at the Art Institute of Chicago], for instance, has such a great feeling, and in a sculpture like *Inner Music,* you just know that you're looking at an artist who had to have had music in him, had to have had dance in him, while working on these male figures (FIG. 13, PLATE 8).

Even though I think we have two major works by Eldzier Cortor (FIG. 14, PLATE 100), I'm still looking for one of his figural compositions with strong angles formed by the position of the arms, the elbows. I'm still searching for better than the ones that we have.

You have to understand that it wasn't just about those artists that exist in their own world. I think you have to look at an artist like Varnette Honeywood, for example, to find a black woman who can get into the humor that we have even while facing adversity. She shows the capacity for humor that is built into every human being, and she is able to put into her art the life, the humor, the warmth, the cuddling, the holding, and the modernization of this life [SEE PLATE 97]. She really brought it in, man. Her works have depth; her work gives you a respite. We don't have the original, but there's a poster of a work by Honeywood that was in the Huxtable house on *The Cosby Show* where the mother is combing the daughter's hair.

ADRIENNE L. CHILDS | I remember that.

fig. 13 | BELOW

[plate 8]
Richmond Barthé
1901–1989, United States
Inner Music
1985
Bronze
58.4 x 23.5 x 27.9 cm
(23 x 9 1/4 x 11 in.)
The Collection of Camille O.
and William H. Cosby Jr.

fig. 14 | OPPOSITE, TOP

[plate 100]
Eldzier Cortor
born 1916, United States
Homage to 466 Cherry Street
1987
Oil on Masonite
93.3 x 118 cm
(36 3/4 x 46 1/2 in.)
The Collection of Camille O.
and William H. Cosby Jr.

fig. 15 | OPPOSITE, BOTTOM

Simmie Knox
born 1935, United States
Wedding Dinner Party
1987
Oil on linen
149.3 x 210.8 x 6.3 cm
(58 3/4 x 83 x 2 1/2 in.)
The Collection of Camille O.
and William H. Cosby Jr.

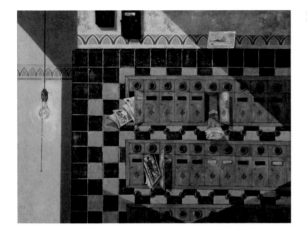

BILL COSBY | Yes! Those times that are painful, but you smile because there was love in what she did, and thank God for her, for her humor that also had warmth and caring. It's like when people say, "Well, it takes a village. . . ." Well, there it is. That's what that village should be about: sitting in that tin tub and getting bathed. There's a feeling of ourselves and who we are.

That brings me to the point about skin tones. A really good artist understands the diversity of skin tones in the African American population. Simmie Knox, for example, is an artist who really gets that. In a family portrait I commissioned, he mastered the skin tones (FIG. 15). This is probably the most challenging piece I have ever given an artist to do. When you look at the placement of the glasses on that table, you can see the artist's approach to design and pattern. In the background, Simmie's color of the Venetian scene (that wallpaper in Aunt Lil and Uncle Jack's house), the expressions on the faces, he did a master's job. And last but not least, the portrait that he did and he actually gave to us, of our son Ennis, the colors in the work and Ennis's expression, he has truly mastered it.

CAMILLE COSBY | The work by Knox is also significant because it focuses on a family, an African American family, and it strikes me as important to represent such a group of people—in this case some of the people are Bill's family members. But it isn't often that one sees works of art that represent African Americans, show our array of skin colors, skin tones, as you see in the painting by Knox. It also appeals to me because it is very colorful.

DRISKELL | I know, Camille, you have been interested in images of black women, African American women—yes, as laborers, but also in other capacities as well. And I remember when I came on board with you all, helping to advise about the collection, that you were always concerned about the balance of the collection in terms of works by a range of African American women artists. There were works by Elizabeth Catlett, of course, but other artists, too.

CAMILLE COSBY | Yes, Alma [Woodsey] Thomas and Loïs Mailou Jones come to mind. I think that we have a good gender balance in our collection, and I'm also aware of the fact that probably most of our collection is before 1980. I think that, too, is important, just as much as the gender balance, to show people that African American artists have been working for a long time. The oldest paintings that we have in our collection date to the late 1700s and early 1800s, with works by the painter Joshua Johnston, who painted portraits of very wealthy white people in Baltimore (FIG. 16, PLATE 5). But see, that's history. It eradicates the myths about African American artists' not being skilled, number one. Number two, it eradicates the myth that they weren't educated, because most of these artists were well educated. They went through four-year institutions or art institutions to be trained.

And in retrospect it has been very important for all of our children to be exposed to our art, because each and every day it reinforces the fact they have a lot to be proud of. It helped them to understand the history of African American people, but it also reinforced them, to mentally counter what has been consistently bombarding them about their definition as a black female or a black male. We have this beautiful little sculpture by William [Ellisworth] Artis, but it's just of a young black male who looks like he is just thinking about something (FIGS. 3, 17, PLATE 36). But nothing ominous, nothing angry looking, as Bill said. It goes against what we see of black males, young black males particularly.

All of our works by black women—Loïs Mailou Jones with her beautiful colorful landscapes, Alma Thomas with all those glorious splashes and dots of color, Faith

fig. 16 | OPPOSITE

[plate 5]
Joshua Johnston
c. 1765–c. 1830, Baltimore
area, Maryland
*Mrs. Thomas Donovan and
Elinor Donovan*
c. 1799
Oil on canvas
76.8 x 64.8 cm
(30 1/4 x 25 1/2 in.)
The Collection of Camille O.
and William H. Cosby Jr.

fig. 17 | RIGHT

[plate 36]
William Ellisworth Artis
1914–1977, United States
African Youth
1940
Bronze
22.2 x 12 x 14 cm
(8 3/4 x 4 3/4 x 5 1/2 in.)
The Collection of Camille O.
and William H. Cosby Jr.

Ringgold's wonderful quilts (FIG. 18, PLATE 106)—are created by women who are very, very significant artists. And they were diverse in terms of what they put on the canvas. There wasn't a similarity pertaining to their imagery.

BILL COSBY | We have many quilts in our collection, some by members of our family. Camille has befriended these women in Mississippi who send her quilts. The quilts tell a story of life, and this is about life without the distractions of radio or TV, without music blaring. Just women sitting with their material, sewing and talking. Quilts tell a story of life, of memory, of family relationships.

CAMILLE COSBY | Speaking of female representations, I also want to focus on the sculptors other than Elizabeth Catlett. Because we have works in the collection by [Mary] Edmonia Lewis, Meta [Vaux] Warrick Fuller, and Augusta Savage. Their works go against the myth that women were not sculptors, and some of those women were sculpting in the 1800s. I just like the fact that we have so much in the collection that will eradicate the myths.

BILL COSBY | It is my understanding that many African American slaves were taught to paint so that the wealthy would have someone to paint their portraits, and these artworks would hang in the home as a result of the slave's exceptional skill. Well, these stories are lost. They're not in the history. When we talk about painting, when we talk about sculpture, we're leaving out facts of history. When you see a building, that architecture is art. And there is a lost truth about African Americans who did the architecture, the drawing, the making of the brick and mortar, and the landscaping. These things are lost, so that we are not included, and if we are not included, it tells the racist society that we can't do such things. We're still working on the brain of the black person in terms of racism. Is that person of equal merit? If they play

fig. 18

[plate 106]
Faith Ringgold
born 1930, United States
*Camille's Husband's
Birthday Quilt* (detail)
1988
Painted and pieced canvas
and silk
269.3 x 207.8 cm
(106 x 81 3/4 in.)
The Collection of Camille O.
and William H. Cosby Jr.

something or do something, are they as good? So when Camille and I started to collect, our uplifting came from the book *Two Centuries of Black American Art* that David Driskell put out in 1976, and then when we sat with David, I accused him of knowing where paintings were hidden, and said that he had stored them on the Underground Railroad so that wherever those slaves were going there was art there to keep them from getting bored.

CHRISTINE MULLEN KREAMER | You mentioned your collection of Shaker furniture. Can you speak about the appeal that Shaker furniture has for you?

CAMILLE COSBY | Now, once again, my husband has been responsible for our Shaker collection. All of the Shaker pieces have been gifts from Bill to me. I love the simplicity of the lines of the Shaker pieces and how utilitarian their histories are. I think that awareness spills over to my taste for African American art, that I like the simplicity. I don't like things that are too busy and ornate. Simplicity, to me, means harmony. So a Shaker piece can be juxtaposed with any of our African American paintings, and they will just blend and be harmonious with each other.

KREAMER | One could also extend that idea of exceptional craftsmanship and harmony of form to beautifully made traditional works of African art.

CAMILLE COSBY | Yes, and for the Shakers, there was a spiritual dimension to work that was done well, something that is equally true for much of Africa's traditional arts.

CHILDS | How do you feel about the fact that you're going to share this collection with so many people? What does it mean to you to share?

BILL COSBY | Don't put your hands on my paintings! *[laughter]*

CAMILLE COSBY | I think it's time. As David knows, we have never allowed any of our works to be exhibited, not as a full collection. And I think it is time, because clearly, since Mr. Obama has become our president, the extremists have shown themselves to be in the forefront. We have always known they were there, but this time they are in your face. I think this is a wonderful time to educate the public about American history, because African American history is American history, and it's important to eradicate the myth that we are monolithic by showing the diversity of African American people through art. So this collection will certainly help to do that.

But when works from our collection are placed in conversation with older, traditional and newer, contemporary African works from the collection of the Smithsonian National Museum of African Art, something wonderful results that has to do with emphasizing a shared emotional and intellectual value of art by artists of color who have something important to say. Some African traditional works were made for utilitarian purposes, others for ceremonial purposes or for bringing beauty into daily life. The aesthetic power of Africa's arts—traditional and contemporary—comes through in this exhibition and complements the African American works from our collection. I think this will be a wonderful educational experience, not educational in a boring sense of the word, but, as Elizabeth Catlett once said, "Art should wake somebody up." We just want people to wake up, and to enjoy themselves while they are awake.

BILL COSBY | One of the important behavioral aspects is that this exhibition at the Smithsonian will also give information to thousands of people who wouldn't ordinarily go someplace and see something like this, although there are galleries and shows all over these United States. There are so many art galleries now that exhibit work by African American artists. For instance, Henry Ossawa Tanner's *The Banjo Lesson* sits at Hampton University Museum in their collection, and because of its popularity, some people make it a point to actually go see it, see it in its frame. It's so important, and in this exhibition here at the Smithsonian National Museum of African Art, people need to rest their eyes upon what we want them to see—it saves them from walking into our house and wearing out the rugs! But, seriously, I think it's important for our young people who are growing in their careers, in their jobs, to know there are places in their cities that show art by African American artists. To me, it's a way to show people what exists, and to give voice to many of these artists who were silenced for so long, some of whom will speak no more.

Perspectives of an Artist and a Curator: A Conversation with David C. Driskell

Adrienne L. Childs

OVER THE COURSE OF several months in 2013, David C. Driskell and Adrienne L. Childs discussed the relationship between African and African American art, the impact of Howard University on Driskell's consciousness as an artist and a scholar, and his experiences as a curator for Bill and Camille Cosby.

ADRIENNE L. CHILDS | The exhibition *Conversations: African and African American Artworks in Dialogue* brings together works of African and African American art in a visual and intellectual dialogue. You consider these connections in your own artistic practice, in your work as a scholar, and in your role as the curator of the Cosby collection of African American art. How did you become interested in the arts of Africa?

DAVID C. DRISKELL | I became interested in African art when I was a student at

Howard University in the early 1950s. This was an exciting time to be there, a golden era in Howard's history as *the* center of black scholarship. It was a place and a time that brought together leading intellectuals whose work focused on Africa, such as the philosopher Alain LeRoy Locke, the historian William Leo Hansberry, and my mentor, James Amos Porter, who was a scholar of both African and African American art. Professor Porter impressed upon me the need to understand both areas of scholarship. So I began my years at Howard by studying painting; then I turned to art history. My artistic practice and my scholarly and curatorial work— over the course of almost six decades—reflect these interrelated pursuits.

Part of my training at Howard involved firsthand experience with works of African art in the university's collection. In a seminar located in a basement classroom of the Founders Library, Professor Porter required that we examine—and handle (with supervision, to be sure!)—works of African art that were in storage or on view in the university art gallery upstairs. I became enamored with African art through this introduction—visual, tactile, intellectual—to actual objects. As a student of art professor Loïs Mailou Jones, I began by sketching masks and other objects, an exercise that required close examination of the forms, volumes, decorative motifs, and materials employed by African artists. Then, in a process somewhat akin to translation into my own idiom, I created paintings, some of which referenced African statuary and masks (SEE FIG. 43, PLATE 11). While some of the other students at Howard engaged in painting still lifes, landscapes, and portraits, I began incorporating African iconography into my work as early as 1953, when I went to study at the Skowhegan School of Painting and Sculpture in Maine as a scholarship participant. Even though I produced many landscapes and still-life paintings there, I also created my own visual vocabulary by incorporating African faces into my compositions (FIG. 20). I realize that these early classroom exercises of engaging

fig. 19 | OVERLEAF

Face mask
Chokwe artist, Democratic
Republic of the Congo,
Angola
Early 20th century
Wood, plant fiber, pigment,
copper alloy
39.1 x 21.3 x 23.5 cm
(15 3/8 x 8 3/8 x 9 1/4 in.)
National Museum of African
Art, Smithsonian Institution,
museum purchase, 85-15-20

fig. 20 | OPPOSITE

David C. Driskell
born 1931, United States
African Fishermen
1953–54
Oil on canvas
61 x 50.8 cm (24 x 20 in.)
Collection of Debbi Reeves

with African works of art was a pedagogical tool designed to awaken in me and in other emerging African American artists studying at Howard a confidence that our work as artists was part of a much longer tradition of creativity and innovation—one that could be traced to Africa.

CHILDS | How did you begin your curatorial work?

DRISKELL | At the same time that I was pursuing my work as a visual artist at Howard, I was honing my curatorial skills. The university art gallery had important works in the collection, including some donated by Dr. Locke, though his larger collection came to the university later. I was fortunate to work as a curatorial assistant to Albert J. Carter, who in 1953 installed the largest assemblage of African art ever to be presented in an exhibition in the city of Washington. The exhibition *African Negro Art* was developed collaboratively by Porter, Hansberry, and

James V. Herring, the chair of the art department. It took place at the Howard University Gallery of Art, and I helped install it. What a privilege! The exhibition included Benin kingdom bronzes and other major works, in all more than two hundred works of African art. Though smaller exhibitions of ten or twelve pieces had been exhibited here and there, nothing on the scale of *African Negro Art* had ever been seen in the city before. In those days the National Museum of the Smithsonian— in the building that's now the National Museum of Natural History, at Tenth and Constitution—had African art on view, but the anthropological displays were old-fashioned and much of the information was inaccurate or outdated. Howard University was the place that one could rely upon to see an accurate depiction of traditional African art—viewed as art. I was fortunate to be there at that time.

CHILDS | Did the exhibition *African Negro Art* and the intellectual life at Howard play a role in discussions to found a museum devoted to African art in Washington?

fig. 21 | OPPOSITE, TOP

Warren M. Robbins in the comparative gallery of the Museum of African Art, A Street NE, c.1963 Eliot Elisofon Photographic Archives, National Museum of African Art, Smithsonian Institution

fig. 22 | OPPOSITE, BOTTOM

Warren M. Robbins in front of the Museum of African Art, A Street NE, c. 1963 Eliot Elisofon Photographic Archives, National Museum of African Art, Smithsonian Institution

fig. 23 | LEFT

The Museum of African Art, A Street NE, c. 1978 Eliot Elisofon Photographic Archives, National Museum of African Art, Smithsonian Institution

DRISKELL | A fair amount has been written about the founding in 1964 of the Museum of African Art, which later became part of the Smithsonian Institution. Seldom does one read, however, about Warren M. Robbins—the founder of the Museum of African Art—coming to Howard University to meet with Porter about his idea to found this museum and to partner with Howard in this endeavor. There was some skepticism at Howard about Robbins's qualifications, as he was a retired Foreign Service officer who lacked academic training in African art and museum practice. When Porter went on leave to Nigeria for a year, and I was serving as acting head of the art department, Robbins paid me a visit to promote his proposal. Despite support from some members of Howard's administration, including the university's then-vice president, Vincent Brown, the joint project did not move forward, and it was clear that the museum was going to be undertaken by Robbins on his own.

Robbins came to the arts of Africa through his appreciation of modern European artists whose work reflected African influences, such as Amedeo Modigliani, Henri Matisse, Juan Gris, and the artists of Die Brücke and Der Blaue Reiter movements (FIG. 21). He recognized that the time was right for such a museum—it was the 1960s and the height of the civil rights movement—and that Washington, D.C., as the seat of the nation's government, was the right place for making a statement about building bridges of cross-cultural communication. In realizing his vision, Robbins set about to build a collection of African and African American art that would serve to inspire dialogue about black artistic accomplishment and its connections to the sources and influences of modernism. In the end, Robbins founded the Museum of African Art on his own, on A Street NE (FIGS. 22, 23), and in 1979 it became a national museum as part of the Smithsonian Institution. The rest, as they say, is history... and my own history with the National Museum of African Art has continued over the years through my service (I now have emeritus status) as a member of the museum's advisory board.

Therefore, although they do not ultimately intersect, the beginnings of the National Museum of African Art and the intellectual climate around African art and African American art at Howard University dovetailed in the 1950s and early 1960s. I think showcasing the Cosby collection with African art here at the Smithsonian National Museum of African Art is almost like coming full circle.

CHILDS | You mention how Warren Robbins came to an appreciation of African art through his connections to modern art. Can you discuss your impressions of the appeal of African art to artists in the West?

DRISKELL | The notion that there is a relationship between African art, modernism, and African American art is an extension of the theory that was promoted in the Harlem Renaissance of looking back while going forward—not unlike the Asante *adinkra* symbol *sankofa,* the bird turning its head back to preen itself, which cues the saying "Go back to fetch it." Its meaning is to look back while strengthening the present and the projections for the future.

My own history reflects this dual engagement—with my artistic practice and my interest in the traditional arts of Africa. Such connections in the West with the arts of Africa have, of course, a much longer history. Certainly, the history of modern European art and the introduction of African art to the American art scene in the early years of the twentieth century were important in terms of the eventual impact on African American artists. It is well known that during the Harlem Renaissance of the 1920s and 1930s, Alain Locke urged artists to look toward modernist use of African art and to the traditional arts of Africa to create what he called a "Negro" idiom, or a style of artistry that uniquely represented black life. Locke saw black Americans as having a relationship to Africa that was ancestral, and by exploring this in the arts they could tap into a form of expression that was true to their heritage. It should be emphasized that one important aspect of the verbal and visual arts of the Harlem Renaissance is that they actively and purposefully looked to Africa as an ancestral inheritance and a source of inspiration. For the first time ideas about African art became intertwined with the ways in which African American artists defined themselves and their artistry. At the time this was quite progressive thinking.

There were, of course, some African cultural practices retained in terms of cultural memory and passed down through generations. When I did the research for the exhibition and publication *Two Centuries of Black American Art* for the Los Angeles County Museum of Art in 1976, for example, the wooden grave markers in Sunbury, Georgia, which were famously documented during the Depression, had just been destroyed, but photographs showed them to be very much like the wooden grave markers that were done in the Congo in the nineteenth century. Another example is the bottle-tree tradition in the South, whereby the branches of trees are decorated with bottles and pottery vessels, and broken pieces of pots and other materials are placed around the tree's base. It suggests a shrine and has a potency to those who understand its visual vocabulary and its connections to Africa.

For African American artists in the twentieth century, I think, the relationship to Africa and African arts is an intellectual choice. If you look at African visual culture, it means being informed by it and seeing a role for it in your own work. That's no different from what Picasso and Modigliani and other European artists did. Yet when African American artists incorporate African art into their work, they run the risk of being accused of copying European modernists. Take my own work: it's not that I am copying Picasso when I introduce African visual elements into my artwork; it is that I am opening myself to African—and other—sources that inspire me in my work. That Picasso was similarly inspired by Africa is a matter of historical timing. Picasso got there ahead of me. He had the advantage of seeing African art before I was born.

CHILDS | How did that legacy of the Harlem Renaissance play out at Howard University?

DRISKELL | I think the legacy of the Harlem Renaissance continued specifically through the discussions and debates that Professors Locke and Porter encouraged through their work. Indeed, they had great disagreements about the role that African art should play in the educational and cultural legacy of African Americans in art. Locke's notion was that the ancestral arts of Africa should be up front, primary, and that artists should literally copy African forms. Porter felt differently; he thought that one should study the works and learn from them, just as the European masters had done. Porter advised that the legacy of African art should be spiritually perceived or absorbed, but not copied. In effect, my work, and the work of so many other African American artists, embraced aspects of these distinctive approaches to knowledge, which are not mutually exclusive but, rather, unite hand and mind as part of the creative process that forges linkages—some obvious, others less so—between Africa and the African diaspora.

For example, Loïs Mailou Jones used African art in her still-life arrangements. Beginning in the 1920s, when she was a student at the School of the Museum of Fine Arts in Boston, Jones studied African art, and she incorporated African iconography into some of her early designs. When Jones went to Paris in 1937, Professor Locke encouraged her to stop painting Parisian scenes and landscapes and to concentrate on African art instead. This resulted in her works *Les Fétiches* (FIG. 24) and *Ascent of Ethiopia* [Milwaukee Art Museum], the latter said to have been inspired by Meta Vaux Warrick Fuller's sculpture *Ethiopia Awakening* [Schomburg Center for Research in Black Culture, New York Public Library]. Rather than put aside French

fig. 24 | OPPOSITE

Loïs Mailou Jones
1905–1998, United States
Les Fétiches
1938
Oil on linen
64.7 x 54 cm
(25 1/2 x 21 1/4 in.)
Smithsonian American Art
Museum, museum purchase
made possible by Mrs.
Norvin H. Green, Dr. R.
Harlan, and Francis
Musgrave, 1990.56

fig. 25 | RIGHT

[plate 50]
Aaron Douglas
1899–1979, United States
Crucifixion
1934
Oil on Masonite
122 x 91.5 cm (48 x 36 in.)
The Collection of Camille O.
and William H. Cosby Jr.

scenes entirely, Jones brought African and other sources of inspiration together in her work. It was her way of honoring Locke's instructions while remaining true to her own artistic vision. As an art professor at Howard University, Jones brought African masks and statuary for us to paint in her watercolor class, recognizing the role of African art in her practice.

Another example one might consider is the work of Aaron Douglas and his approach to cubism. Douglas's acceptance of modernism and his connections to African art came through the German painter Winold Reiss. When they met in New York in 1924, Douglas was still doing portraits. Reiss suggested that Douglas should try to connect to African art in his own way, not necessarily the way Picasso did. Thus, rather than portraying multiple views at once, Douglas worked with a hard-edged, flattened form of cubism that was more akin to Mondrian's (FIG. 25, PLATE 50).

Locke, as the father of black American art criticism, encouraged Douglas to look to Africa for inspiration. Douglas adhered to that principle better than any other artist of the time. He artistically went "back to Africa" by putting African scenes in finished murals that he did at the Schomburg Center (the 135th Street branch of the New York Public Library at the time). In this and other work, Douglas was adhering to the principles that Locke promoted, which sought to preserve the ancestral legacy by re-creating forms that echoed African sensibilities. As I mentioned earlier, James Porter thought that was somewhat superficial. That is where Porter and Locke disagreed and that's where Porter and Douglas disagreed.

Douglas went to Africa in the 1950s. Other African Americans were there when Léopold Senghor went to Europe in the 1920s. They were in Paris in the 1930s when Négritude was born. They were all in search of "What is Africa to me?" This all-important question, which was posed by the Harlem Renaissance poet Countee Cullen in his 1925 poem "Heritage," sought to place the children of the African diaspora within what I have called elsewhere a "racially empowered comfort zone" that encouraged a creative understanding of their relationship to the great cultural traditions of the continent of Africa.

CHILDS | How did you come to work with Bill and Camille Cosby, and how would you characterize your role in shaping the Cosby collection of African American art?

DRISKELL | I began as curator of the Cosby collection in January of 1978. I was contacted first in October of 1977 by Bill, who invited me and my wife, Thelma, to come and spend the Thanksgiving holiday with them. I did not know them except by Bill's profession as an entertainer. So when he called me that day, I asked him why he was requesting my service. He responded by saying, "I have what they tell me is the black bible on art, *Two Centuries of Black American Art,* and I've been told if we want someone to help us build an important collection, then you are the person." Our association began with that.

Our visit to the Cosby home was to look at what they had in the collection at that time. They had quite a few works by the African American artists Charles White and William Pajaud, but their collection was comprised mainly of works by European American artists such as the modernists Stuart Davis and Reginald Marsh, and Worthington Whittredge, a nineteenth-century landscape painter. (There were no African American landscape painters from that era in the Cosby collection at that time.) The collection also included a Hackensack Valley scene by George Inness,

fig. 26

Claude Clark
1915–2001, United States,
Sponge Fisherman
1944
Oil on board
46.3 x 62.3 cm
(18 1/4 x 24 1/2 in.)
The Collection of Camille O.
and William H. Cosby Jr.

as well as works by Maurice Prendergast and the American social-realist painter Thomas Hart Benton. It was mainly a collection of fine-quality works by European American artists. My responsibility was, from day one, to expand their collection to include quality works by African Americans, and to look at a broader historical overview of what they should be collecting. I am not aware of any other collectors embarking on such an endeavor of this scale and with the amount of resources that were potentially available to build a world-class collection of African American art.

It was very exciting. I had recently moved to the University of Maryland, from having spent ten years teaching at Fisk University in Nashville and serving as chair of the Department of Art and director of the gallery. It was from Fisk that I curated the *Two Centuries* exhibition. We were excited about the possibility of expanding the Cosby collection, looking at the work of other artists and bringing in new names and talents to their collection. When I came on board, I immediately started focusing their attention on nineteenth-century artists such as Robert S. Duncanson, Edward Mitchell Bannister, Henry Ossawa Tanner, Mary Edmonia Lewis, and others. The Cosbys were receptive to the notion. One of my basic responsibilities was to get in touch with people and sources whereby we could bring a number of new works into the collection.

At that initial meeting at their home, Camille and Bill Cosby communicated to me the notion that they wanted American art that reflected the African American experience. At that time they were interested in the black visual experience in America, mainly in the narrative portrayal of it through figural art (FIG. 26).

The lineage of the production by African American artists is important for the record, and for building a collection that reflects this history. One begins with Joshua Johnston, because he is the primary figure who has been documented in the art history of early African American artists (SEE FIG. 16, PLATE 5). The acquisition by the Cosbys of Johnston's *Lady on a Red Sofa* (FIGS. 27, 56, PLATE 28) was important—it had been shown and published in *Two Centuries*. It was owned by Peter Tillou, a Connecticut dealer and collector. I knew where it was, and I was listening for information about artworks that I knew would fit the Cosbys' collecting interests. There were very few cases when my recommendations were rebuffed by Camille and Bill, because I knew their tastes and I wasn't trying to promote my own agenda.

Their main interest was the American scene, not so much the African scene, though they appreciated my passion for African art. One of my responsibilities as a cultural adviser and curator to the Cosbys was to help give direction to the education of the Cosby children. And that meant, in some cases, taking them to Africa and other places. Bill never went along, but Camille often traveled with us. We traveled to Europe, the Middle East, Africa, and South America. The Cosbys had an expansive view of world cultures and traveled with their family, but their collecting practices really centered on African American art.

CHILDS | Were the Cosbys proposing a political or moral point of view in building a collection that emphasized the image of the black figure, and black culture, in a positive, uplifting way?

DRISKELL | Yes, I would say to a certain extent that there was a political but also, importantly, a cultural agenda in the approach the Cosbys took to building their collection. They didn't profess to know the precise points of that history; they left that very much up to me. But I knew they wanted their collection to reflect images of

fig. 27 | OPPOSITE

[plate 28]
Joshua Johnston
c. 1765–c. 1830,
Baltimore area, Maryland
Lady on a Red Sofa
c. 1825
Oil on canvas
76.8 x 64.8 cm
(30 1/4 x 25 1/2 in.)
The Collection of Camille O.
and William H. Cosby Jr.

dignity and an uplifting of the race. They didn't want artworks depicting downtrodden-looking individuals, like some of the works by nineteenth-century white artists that tended to patronize black subjects. They wanted positive imagery created by important, skilled African American artists, and that's what I tried to bring to them. And in some cases, they saw a work ahead of me, and said, "Go get that."

I never had a figure for the budget. It was always, "Tell us what you find, and we will look at it and see whether or not it's possible." And on no occasion can I recall having been turned down from purchasing something. Bill once said, "There are going to be times when you as the curator will wish to exercise your judgment about what should be collected. You know the ins and outs about collecting, saying what we should have in the collection. I'm the entertainer, and I'm the person who will be the recipient of your knowledge. There are going to be times when you will want to buy something for the collection, that you think it should be a part of our collection, and I'm going to say no." He then said, "You want to know why?" And I said, "Yes! I'd like to know why." He said, "Because it's my money." My retort was, "Okay, just don't hold me responsible later on for something that you decided you wanted to purchase, when I have already advised you of another work that you should have."

CHILDS | Was it hard to find African American art of good quality during those years?

DRISKELL | No, remember this was the late 1970s, and a lot of the works were just being unveiled to the American public. I had recently revealed this to some in 1976 through my *Two Centuries* exhibition and book, which featured a treasure trove of African American art, much of it of exceptionally high quality, that had never been seen before in public. That was the response from so many people. When they saw the quality of the work by Duncanson, Bannister, and Tanner, they asked, "Where have these artists and artworks been, and what have we been looking at? What's going on?" Much of this was new to them and it was gratifying to me to be able to point this out. Here was a large body of work by African American artists that's as good as any that's been created: Duncanson being considered a second-generation Hudson River school painter; Bannister painting in the mood of the Barbizon painters (FIG. 28). These were revelations for some, as so few people knew about their work. With the exception of what my Howard University professor James Porter had written about these artists, few knew much at all about these works. No one could argue rationally—and honestly—if they maintained that such works were not as good as, say, those of Whittredge. Yes, they were. Here was Bannister, who had received a bronze medal at the 1876 Centennial Exposition in Philadelphia. As you know, he had to receive the medal without honor because they didn't think that any black person had the intellectual capacity to produce such works. My *Two Centuries* exhibition and publication, and the Cosbys' collecting interests, refuted such notions.

The process of building the collection included networking with individual collectors and dealers. Edward Shein, from Providence, Rhode Island, was one of the dealers who was particularly helpful, as he had been collecting African American artworks for many years. He knew where these works were located. In some cases we went to Shein to make purchases, and in other cases we went directly to collectors. It was on that basis that we were able to single out a pool of works and start adding them to the collection.

CHILDS | Was it like curating an exhibition?

DRISKELL | I wasn't thinking along the same lines as curating an exhibition, but in building the Cosby collection, I wanted to identify the same quality of first-class

fig. 28
Edward Mitchell Bannister
1828–1901, Canada
Homestead
1883
Oil on canvas
86.3 x 111.8 cm (34 x 44 in.)
The Collection of Camille O.
and William H. Cosby Jr.

works that a curator would select for an exhibition. I knew the works were out there. To a certain extent, I wanted to mirror my own tastes in the importance of showing a historical record. I wanted that record to be reflected in the Cosby collection, and I felt that they should collect the very best. Here was a chance to collect stellar art, and money was not a problem; I was told that. But I did not have carte blanche; everything had to be passed by Camille and Bill to make sure that it fit their collective and individual tastes.

The Cosby collection reflects my own vision of what a major collection of African American art should be. I guess I saw myself as the Bernard Berenson of the African American art world. Here I am, advising the Cosbys the way Berenson advised Isabella Stewart Gardner in Boston. That's probably not a good analogy, but I don't know anybody else who's done it in such a direct and hands-on manner. It was research and legwork, pursuing things, going here and there, making enlightened decisions.

fig. 29

[plate 141]
Archibald J. Motley Jr.
1891–1981, United States
Stomp
1927
Oil on canvas
76.3 x 91.5 cm (30 x 36 in.)
The Collection of Camille O.
and William H. Cosby Jr.

For example, I purchased the Motley works at a time when his work was not being highly collected. I went to Chicago to collect two works in 1979. Archibald J. Motley Jr. was still very active, and when I was there he was painting a work he called *The First 100 Years* [private collection], which included a conglomeration of references, including imagery of Dr. Martin Luther King Jr. Artists often feel that their current work is their best, and Motley felt that *The First 100 Years* was better than the two works I had selected for the Cosby collection: *Stomp* (FIGS. 29, 108, PLATE 141) and *Bronzeville at Night* (SEE PLATE 142). I explained that the Cosbys wished to acquire works in the artist's signature style, which is why I chose the works I did. Motley died in 1981, so I was fortunate to acquire for the Cosbys two significant works from this important artist.

Other works came to the Cosby collection as part of public auction. That was the case with the acquisition of Tanner's masterpiece, *The Thankful Poor* (SEE FIG. 67, PLATE 47). The painting had been owned by the Pennsylvania School for the Deaf in Philadelphia; it is my understanding that the artist had given it to the school. On December 10, 1981, it was put up for sale at Sotheby's, then located on Madison Avenue in New York. *The Thankful Poor* had not been seen in public for a long time, and there hadn't been much in the popular press about it. In preparation for the sale, I asked Camille Cosby, "Do I have a budget? Do I have a limit?" And she replied, "I want the painting for Bill's Christmas gift. Get the painting." And I did.

CHILDS | Was there anyone else bidding against you?

DRISKELL | Yes. There were two other people bidding against me, but I knew that they had a limit. It sold for $250,000 plus commission, which brought it up to $287,000. That was the highest price that had ever been paid at auction for a work by an African American artist at that time.

CHILDS | Tell me more about the collection . . . some highlights from your perspective?

DRISKELL | Camille and Bill Cosby were also interested in acquiring works by African American artists whose art demonstrated technical mastery and approaches to subject matter and themes that had long been part of the canon of Western artistic production—portraits, landscapes, religious subject matter, still-life compositions, and so on. They were convinced, and rightly so, that accomplished African American artists were part of American art history but that their contributions had been overlooked by virtue of the fact that they were black. By focusing their collecting attentions on artworks by African Americans, they hoped to bring well-deserved attention to these long-neglected individuals and to demonstrate to artists and collectors alike that there was a market for quality works created by African Americans.

Their acquisition of a work like Aaron Douglas's *Crucifixion,* for example, makes a powerful statement about black spirituality and changing the dominant Western narrative of Christianity (FIG. 25, PLATE 50). It was very controversial for Douglas, and later for William Henry Johnson, to depict Christian themes with African and African American themes, because nobody thought of depicting God as black. If you look at Douglas's *Crucifixion,* the interesting thing is that the Christ figure is one of the smallest figures in the whole composition. Simon of Cyrene, the African who bears the cross, is a much more powerfully rendered figure. Even the Roman soldiers around them seem more important than the Christ figure—a marked contrast to Western depictions of the Crucifixion. By focusing on Simon of Cyrene as the principal figure, Douglas was emphasizing an African connection and making a point about slavery and the building of America by black folks. Douglas was quite a politician when it came to his art. He wanted his art to teach and change and to tell stories, to be narrative, but in ways that changed the dominant Western narrative to one that emphasized a focus on black contributions. Indeed, I had Douglas in mind when I did the stained-glass east windows in 1991 at the Peoples Congregational United Church of Christ in Washington, D.C. In my window there is no overt Christ figure. The figure is both Simon of Cyrene and Jesus, but the figure is depicted as a slave (FIG. 30). Much of my philosophy comes from Douglas.

fig. 30

David C. Driskell
born 1931, United States
East window of the Peoples
Congregational United
Church of Christ, Washington, D.C.
1991
Faceted glass, cement
Diam: 426.8 cm (168 in.)

fig. 31

[plate 52]
Minnie Evans
1892–1987, United States
Design Made at Airlie Garden
1969
Oil and mixed media on
canvas board
41.3 x 57.8 cm
(16 1/4 x 22 3/4 in.)
The Collection of Camille O.
and William H. Cosby Jr.

A different approach to spiritual subject matter can be seen in the work of Minnie Evans (FIGS. 31, 70, PLATE 52), who portrays faces and figures in a manner similar to the ways that African carvers fashioned masks and figures: they are frontal, they look you right in the face, they are meant to confront you and make you engage. That is what the mask does, it centralizes the concept (SEE FIG. 19). The idea of spirituality is further emphasized by the focus on the head, not the soul, as the seat of wisdom in African thought. In the West we often reference, in Gospel music, "my heart, my soul is anchored in the Lord." In my understanding, it is the mind that is anchored in African thought, an idea symbolized by the importance of the head as the seat of wisdom (SEE PLATE 77).

As one who had experienced the horrors of World War I, Horace Pippin was very much concerned with notions of peace. His work addressed age-old questions: How do we get along? How do we erase warfare? Pippin turned to the Bible, to the Peaceable Kingdom, as his guide (FIGS. 32, 69, PLATE 49). His work, the three-part Holy Mountain series, was keyed to ideas found in scriptural references: "The lamb shall lie down with the lion"; "We shall beat our swords into ploughshares, and we shall study war no more"; "Gonna lay down my sword and shield down by the riverside and study war no more." Pippin's shepherd in *The Holy Mountain I* is black, and of course he is the Good Shepherd, a Christ figure. Pippin saw black people as part and parcel of biblical narrative.

Much of that comes out of a time when black people were engaged in a direct dialogue with God, a process of talking directly to God so that they could be relieved of their human misery on earth. This was a carryover from the experience of slavery, the recognition of the enslaved that nobody else would listen to them, and that white people did not even want them in their churches. As a result they founded their own churches, and in doing so, they became very, very close to God. How? In song, in dance, and in verse—that's how spirituality was communicated in black churches, and these ideas were explored in different ways by William Henry Johnson, Archibald Motley Jr., Horace Pippin, and other African American artists who depicted spiritual or religious subject matter.

Emphasizing African American agency in religious practice was at the heart of works by these and other African American artists. Margo Humphrey, for example, countered her upbringing in the Lutheran faith—a non-black Protestant tradition—by Africanizing, if you will, certain iconic Christian subject matter, as in *The Last Bar-B-Que* (FIGS. 33, 71, PLATE 53), which was Humphrey's take on the Last Supper, or by incorporating pyramids and other ancient Egyptian imagery into her work. Humphrey borrowed imagery from India and elsewhere, demonstrating her commitment to appropriating whatever religious subject matter suited her purpose. There was clarity in the contradictions she set up in her work, and an assertion that African American religious experience could be part of a more universal experience.

These ideas about black spirituality, of black agency in religious practice, were—and remain—of interest to Camille and Bill Cosby. They recognize the role of religion in African

fig. 32 | LEFT

[plate 49]
Horace Pippin
1888–1946, United States
The Holy Mountain I (detail)
1944
Oil on canvas
76.2 x 91.5 cm (30 x 36 in.)
The Collection of Camille O. and William H. Cosby Jr.

fig. 33 | BELOW

[plate 53]
Margo Humphrey
born 1942, United States
The Last Bar-B-Que (detail)
1988
Lithograph
66 x 96.5 cm (26 x 38 in.)
The Collection of Camille O. and William H. Cosby Jr.

fig. 34 | ABOVE

[plate 33]
Charles White
1918–1979, United States
*Homage to Langston
Hughes* (detail)
1971
Oil on canvas
122 x 122 cm (48 x 48 in.)
The Collection of Camille O.
and William H. Cosby Jr.

fig. 35 | RIGHT

[plate 32]
Charles White
1918–1979, United States
Seed of Heritage
1968
Ink on illustration board
152.5 x 114.3 cm
(60 x 45 in.)
The Collection of Camille O.
and William H. Cosby Jr.

American life, but they are equally cognizant that its expression in black communities was linked to complex histories that bypassed the sufferings of people of color and kept African Americans on the margins of mainstream religious practice. It's not surprising, then, that their collection includes works by African American artists who address these issues in subtle and not so subtle ways. They were, you might say, interested in African American stories that were told by the artists whose works they collected.

In addition to collecting works that explored aspects of black spirituality, Camille and Bill Cosby gravitated toward other themes that reflected their own strong interests in family, history, memory, gender, and identity, and how these were explored and aesthetically resolved in works by African American artists. Charles White's heroic figures, for example, are very important in terms of the fashioning of a black aesthetic around ideas of black personhood (FIGS. 34, 48, PLATE 33). In his powerful depictions of women and men, his point of view is "African American," and by using that terminology I mean that he sees connections to Africa through his explorations of the black experience. White said that throughout his life he was trying to paint just one picture, a picture about the beauty and the positive aspects of the black experience. It's not surprising, then, that one of the first works of African American art acquired by the Cosbys is a magnificent maternity figure by Charles White, a work that remains a particular favorite with Camille, who is drawn to the idea—and the image—of strong women (FIGS. 35, 58, PLATE 32).

The Cosby collection also includes important works by Elizabeth Catlett. I think the Cosbys responded to how Elizabeth Catlett was cognizant of the notion of a black aesthetic, and that she worked toward the creation of a formal approach that reflected that aesthetic. Catlett was connecting to her own history by incorporating African and pre-Colombian traditional forms into her compositions of men, women, and children. When people asked Catlett what she was trying to do in her work, she would reply with her motto, "Art should wake somebody up." Catlett was trying to wake people up, to let them see that they were still enslaved, still segregated, still "Jim Crowed," still under the whip, whether they wanted to admit it or not. There was a consciousness that Catlett wanted to instill through her work. Her work was not about depictions of pretty black folk but about works that grabbed you in a visceral way and made a political point about endowing the black mind with an understanding of the roots of black identity and about the relationship to other people of color.

Camille and Bill Cosby didn't begin to collect Catlett's work until the 1980s, however, and they were all commissioned pieces. I went to Catlett's studio first in 1983, to start working with the artist on artworks for the Cosby collection. The Cosbys were specific with their instructions. The process went along the lines of Bill calling me and saying, "I want you to go to Mexico to visit Miss Catlett. For Camille's birthday, I want a figure that shows a very sophisticated lady. I want something that captures her beauty and her strength." Or, "I want something that captures the essence of the entire family." The result is a beautiful, massive work, *The Family,* which captures all of the family symbolically within the embrace of love (FIG. 36, PLATE 34). Through my discussions with Bill and Camille Cosby, I would come to understand what they wished to achieve in a particular commissioned work. I would discuss their ideas with Catlett. She would then take it from there and realize their ideas beautifully in her own inimitable way.

The Cosby collection also reflects a keen interest in African American history. Jacob Lawrence is a history painter. Even when he is recording what's going on in the streets of Harlem, that's history of a given time or period. It's a temporal kind of

fig. 36 | OPPOSITE

[plate 34]
Elizabeth Catlett
1915–2012, United States
The Family
1983–84
Marble
163.8 x 45.7 x 44.5 cm
(64 1/2 x 18 x 17 1/2 in.)
The Collection of Camille O.
and William H. Cosby Jr.

fig. 37 | RIGHT

[plate 143]
Jacob Lawrence
1917–2000, United States
Blind Musician
1942
Gouache
53.3 x 73.8 cm (21 x 29 in.)
The Collection of Camille O.
and William H. Cosby Jr.

thing, and his compositions of black musicians and street scenes capture very special moments at a time when black people hadn't yet accepted themselves as being necessarily, importantly black (FIGS. 37, 109, PLATE 143). It wasn't really until the cultural revolution of the 1960s that there was widespread recognition that "black is beautiful"—an understanding that Stokely Carmichael didn't invent, but it took a movement to popularize it. People started seeing themselves as black and beautiful in the 1960s, even though Langston Hughes had written about it in his 1940 poem "Note on Commercial Theatre," when he said:

> *But someday somebody'll*
> *Stand up and talk about me,*
> *And write about me—*
> *Black and beautiful—*
>
> . . . .
>
> *I reckon it'll be*
> *Me myself!*
>
> *Yes, it'll be me.* [1]

fig. 38 | LEFT

Bob Thompson
1937–1966, United States
Horse and Blue Rider
1965
Oil on canvas
35.5 x 45.8 cm (14 x 18 in.)
The Collection of Camille O.
and William H. Cosby Jr.

fig. 39 | OPPOSITE

[plate 118]
Bob Thompson
1937–1966, United States
Bird with Nudes
1964
Oil on canvas
92 x 122 cm (36 1/4 x 48 in.)
The Collection of Camille O.
and William H. Cosby Jr.

CHILDS | Were the Cosbys interested in avant-garde art? Did you ever try to lead them in collecting directions that they resisted?

DRISKELL | The avant-garde was not generally part of the collecting taste of Camille and Bill Cosby. However, they were very interested in the unusual Beat-generation painter Bob Thompson, and they have collected many of his works (FIGS. 38, 39, 100, PLATE 118). They also acquired a work by the 1980s contemporary artist Jean-Michel Basquiat, who brought together graffiti, jazz, and hip-hop (SEE PLATE 12). Although Thompson and Basquiat are unconventional, to say the least, their works are consistent with the Cosbys' collecting interests in imagery focusing on the human figure.

I encouraged them to branch out a bit and include more abstract works in their collection. During the years that they were actively building their collection, they moved toward abstraction in the work of Charles Alston (FIG. 41, PLATE 30) and Romare Bearden (SEE FIG. 104, PLATE 146). They have since included works by abstract artists such as Martin Puryear (SEE PLATE 54) and Alma Woodsey Thomas (FIG. 42; SEE PLATE 120).

Alma Thomas's color-field painting tapped into a universal pattern, a worldview. She was studying painting with Robert Gates at American University in Washington, D.C. She and Sam Gilliam were part of the second-generation color-field painters. To my knowledge, there was no African consciousness intended in her work. You could tie it visually to African textile patterns, I suppose, but I never heard Alma say she was looking at African art or textiles in any way. Cognizant of the Washington Color school, Thomas moved out of conventional representational painting into forms of abstraction that were patterned, but with patterns and lines that were deliberately fractured or broken up in some way. She used color to break the forms, and in using color, she was looking at Kenneth Noland, Morris Louis, Howard Mehring, and Leon Berkowitz.

CHILDS | What about political themes, such as those explored in the work of Robert Colescott?

DRISKELL | Yes, Colescott's *Death of a Mulatto Woman* (FIGS. 40, 78, PLATE 69) was about as close as Camille and Bill Cosby got to works that were infused with overt political subject matter. What you have to remember about Colescott is that he is seminal in that kind of double consciousness of black imagery. In a way, Colescott was poking fun at the history of black imagery, but he was also telling us to read history, to learn from it. But I don't think Camille and Bill Cosby were ever interested in blatant political art, art that made a stark political statement. One could say that Charles White's art makes a political statement, if one considers images of dignity political. Similarly, African American artists working with other themes—such as black spirituality—were inserting people of color into white-dominated narratives, so simply creating religiously themed art or idealized landscapes inspired by literary works could be viewed as subtle political statements critiquing the status quo.

　　That, no doubt, was part of the appeal to Camille and Bill Cosby, whose collection demonstrates, conclusively, that exceptionally talented African American artists deserve their place in the history of American, and global, art.

fig. 40

[plate 69]
Robert Colescott
1925–2009, United States
Death of a Mulatto Woman
(detail)
1991
Acrylic on canvas
213.3 x 182.8 cm
(84 x 72 in.)
The Collection of Camille O.
and William H. Cosby Jr.

NOTE

1. Langston Hughes, "Note on Commercial Theatre,"
in Hughes 1995, 216.

fig. 41 | RIGHT

[plate 30]
Charles Alston
1907–1977, United States
Woman and Child
c. 1955
Oil on canvas
127 x 91.5 cm (50 x 36 in.)
The Collection of Camille O.
and William H. Cosby Jr.

fig. 42 | FAR RIGHT

Alma Woodsey Thomas
1891–1978, United States
Azaleas Extravaganza
1968
Acrylic on canvas
183 x 132 cm (72 x 52 in.)
The Collection of Camille O.
and William H. Cosby Jr.

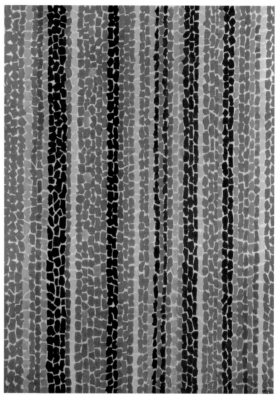

Conversations Considered: Curators and Objects in Dialogue

Christine Mullen Kreamer and Adrienne L. Childs

CONVERSATIONS: *African and African American Artworks in Dialogue* recognizes the communicative and visual potency of works of art. Although created for distinct purposes by artists who are often separated from one another by vast distances of time and space, works of African and African American art can be brought together in a visual and intellectual dialogue to explore particular themes.

In this exhibition there are multiple approaches—curatorial, artistic, and personal—to the idea of conversations. As a scholarly endeavor, the selection of artworks and their organization according to particular themes reflects conversations among the members of the curatorial team,[1] who bring particular subject-area expertise to the distinct fields of African and African American art history. Curatorial decisions, informed by scholarship, are subjective and directed toward engaging particular points of view. The curatorial endeavor, however, begins with the object, which provides the focal point for intellectual, visual, and aesthetic contemplation.

So when presented with the unprecedented opportunity to place works of African art from the collection of the National Museum of African Art in dialogue with African American artworks from the Cosby collection, the curators began by selecting the best works from each collection as a step toward identifying points of interconnection. It was important to establish the scope and depth of the Cosby collection in terms of time, media, and subject matter. Thus the team chose artworks that range from a late eighteenth-century portrait by Joshua Johnston (FIG. 16, PLATE 5) to mid-nineteenth-century landscapes by Robert S. Duncanson (FIG. 2, PLATE 6), to works by the late nineteenth-century artist Henry Ossawa Tanner (FIG. 45, PLATE 7), to paintings of daily life that formed part of early and mid-twentieth-century art movements. The collection also includes commissioned artworks, such as the sculptures from the 1980s by Elizabeth Catlett (PLATE 13), and work by abstract and more avant-garde artists, including Jean-Michel Basquiat (PLATE 12). As Bill and Camille Cosby have noted (see "Collecting Priorities," this volume), their conversations with the artist, scholar, and curator of their collection, David C. Driskell, concentrated on their determination to acquire works of high quality by African American artists that suited their collecting sensibilities. Their taste tends to favor works that are American-centric, have bold color schemes, depict in a naturalistic way positive, uplifting subject matter, and explore the range of African American experiences. Once the African American works from the Cosby collection

fig. 43 | OVERLEAF, LEFT
[plate 11]
David C. Driskell
born 1931, United States
Benin Head
c. 1978
Egg tempera on paper
19 x 19 cm (7 1/2 x 7 1/2 in.)
The Collection of Camille O.
and William H. Cosby Jr.

fig. 44 | OVERLEAF, RIGHT
[plate 1]
Edo artist, Benin kingdom
court style, Nigeria
Commemorative head of
a king
18th century
Copper alloy, iron
33 x 23.5 x 23.2 cm
(13 x 9 1/4 x 9 1/8 in.)
National Museum of African
Art, Smithsonian Institution,
gift of Joseph H. Hirshhorn
to the Smithsonian Institution
in 1979, 85-19-16

fig. 45

[plate 7]
Henry Ossawa Tanner
1859–1937, United States
Study of an Arab
1897
Oil on board
33 x 24 cm (13 x 9 1/2 in.)
The Collection of Camille O.
and William H. Cosby Jr.

were selected, the team set about determining thematic connections with particular African artworks from the museum's collection.

In developing the theme of *Conversations,* the curatorial team was cognizant of the need to avoid making facile connections based solely on visual similarities, which would inadvertently and incorrectly have essentialized the material and have suggested—again incorrectly—that African American artists are naturally drawn to or connected with African art by virtue of their race and their ancestral heritage from the African continent. This is not the case; rather, it is a conscious decision by some, not all, African American artists (and other artists, for that matter) to connect in their work—in a diversity of ways—to Africa. There are points of synchronicity and convergence, as well as divergence, in the dialogues established through the juxtapositions of African and African American works of art. Furthermore, the works chosen for *Conversations* allow us to consider the ways African American artists depict and offer up ways of being African American/diasporan and ways of seeing African American/diasporan culture. The same may be said for the African artworks on view, which offer multiple points of entry into the ways that artists and their artworks communicate rich and complex messages about the social, economic, political, and aesthetic value of art within and outside Africa. Thus the connections made in the selection and thematic grouping of artworks—African and African American—assembled for *Conversations* are substantive ones.

David Driskell's painting *Benin Head* (FIG. 43, PLATE 11) for example, is in dialogue with the long history of art making on the African continent, for it deliberately references masterful, centuries-old copper-alloy castings by Edo artists working in Nigeria's Benin kingdom (FIG. 44, PLATE 1). Driskell's understanding of African art (see "Perspectives of an Artist and a Curator," this volume) is reflected in his focus on the head in communicating attributes of ethnic identity and status but also as a locus of spiritual power—something that the artist captures exceedingly well in the penetrating eyes of his subject. The artist's connections to Africa and African art were forged during his studies in the 1950s at Howard University in Washington, D.C., where the philosopher Alain LeRoy Locke and the artists James Amos Porter and James Lesene Wells encouraged their students to embrace African art as a source of inspiration in their work. Indeed, the colorful palettes and subject matter employed in Porter's *Washerwoman* (FIG. 46, PLATE 9) and Wells's *Georgetown Garden* (FIG. 47, PLATE 10) no doubt mirror ideas about the presentation of self and the dignity of work and its contributions to family and community that resonated with African Americans—but that apply equally to experiences in African communities.

The organizational framework of the exhibition reflects broad and interconnected themes that are central to artworks over time and around the globe. They are not uniquely the purview of African and African American art. Rather, the themes resonate with the experiences of people the world over, and thus they form a point of connection to works of art that may be unfamiliar to some when they first enter the exhibition or peruse this book. A quick glance at the works of art assembled for *Conversations* reveals that the human form has been a major source of inspiration for both African and African American artists in their explorations of personhood, gender, identity, status, spirituality, history, memory, and creativity. The messages encoded in the representations of the human form, however, may be distinct, reflecting deeply personal ideas or, conversely, shared and culture-specific aesthetic concepts. The same can be said for the other themes—spiritualities; power and politics; memory, family, and the domestic sphere; nature as metaphor; music and urban culture—that are explored in *Conversations* and discussed in the essays that follow.

The artworks themselves engage us in a different manner, as they were created by

fig. 46
[plate 9]
James Amos Porter
1905–1970, United States
Washerwoman
n.d.
Oil on canvas
45.8 x 33 cm (18 x 13 in.)
The Collection of Camille O.
and William H. Cosby Jr.

fig. 47

[plate 10]
James Lesesne Wells
1902–1993, United States
Georgetown Garden
1958
Oil on canvas
48.3 x 55.9 cm (19 x 22 in.)
The Collection of Camille O.
and William H. Cosby Jr.

talented artists who communicate via a visual language of form, color, texture, material, and imagery. Effective use of this visual language draws our eye and our mind to ideas that artists hope to convey, thereby encouraging us to pursue lines of inquiry regarding the technique, imagery, and/or meaning of the works. Ultimately, great works of art prompt us to look closely, to discern visual elements that communicate meaning, message, and artistic intent, to form our own ideas about an artwork and its relevance to our lives, and to be moved by the aesthetic experience that art offers us all.

Conversations thus looks both toward the past and toward the future. In dialogue with selected works of African art from the collection of the Smithsonian National Museum of African Art, the works by African American artists from the Cosby collection reflect and refract a dynamic artistic conversation. This colloquy encourages all of us to draw from the wellspring of creativity that is Africa, to recognize the shared histories that inextricably link Africa and the African diaspora to the wider world, and to seek the common threads that over time weave our stories together into the narrative of the human family.

NOTE

1. The *Conversations* team is made up of David C. Driskell, artist, scholar, and curator, and Adrienne L. Childs, independent scholar, who are both specialists in African American art, as well as Africanist art historians Christine Mullen Kreamer, deputy director and chief curator, and Bryna Freyer, curator, at the Smithsonian National Museum of African Art. The museum's director, Johnnetta Betsch Cole, knowledgeable about both African and African American art, served as adviser throughout the organization of the exhibition and publication.

plate 1
_____

Edo artist, Benin kingdom
court style, Nigeria
Commemorative head of
a king
18th century
Copper alloy, iron
33 x 23.5 x 23.2 cm
(13 x 9 1/4 x 9 1/8 in.)
National Museum of African
Art, Smithsonian Institution,
gift of Joseph H. Hirshhorn
to the Smithsonian Institution
in 1979, 85-19-16

plate 2

Kongo artist, Angola,
Democratic Republic of
the Congo, Republic of
the Congo
Female figure with child
(niongi)
Late 19th to early 20th
century
Wood, pigment, mirror
glass
54 x 27.9 x 26.4 cm
(21 1/4 x 11 x 10 3/8 in.)
National Museum of African
Art, Smithsonian Institution,
gift of the Eugene and
Agnes E. Meyer Founda-
tion, 72-41-4

plate 3
_____

Alamide
active c. 1925–50, Yoruba
artist, Nigeria
Gelede mask
1925–50
Wood, pigment
20.9 x 19.1 x 33.3 cm
(8 1/4 x 7 1/2 x 13 1/8 in.)
National Museum of African
Art, Smithsonian Institution,
gift of Ernst Anspach, 96-6-4

plate 4

Unidentified artist,
Bondoukou area,
Côte d'Ivoire
Female figure
Early to mid-20th century
Wood
42.6 x 5.5 x 4.5 cm
(16 3/4 x 2 3/16 x 1 3/4 in.)
National Museum of African
Art, Smithsonian Institution,
gift of Evelyn A. J. Hall and
John A. Friede, 85-8-5

plate 5 | LEFT

Joshua Johnston
c. 1765–c. 1830,
Baltimore area, Maryland
*Mrs. Thomas Donovan and
Elinor Donovan*
c. 1799
Oil on canvas
76.8 x 64.8 cm
(30 1/4 x 25 1/2 in.)
The Collection of Camille O.
and William H. Cosby Jr.

plate 6 | OPPOSITE

Robert S. Duncanson
1821–1872, United States
Vale of Kashmir
1864
Oil on canvas
45.8 x 76.5 cm
(18 x 30 1/8 in.)
The Collection of Camille O.
and William H. Cosby Jr.

plate 7

Henry Ossawa Tanner
1859–1937, United States
Study of an Arab
1897
Oil on board
33 x 24 cm (13 x 9 1/2 in.)
The Collection of Camille O.
and William H. Cosby Jr.

plate 8

Richmond Barthé
1901–1989, United States
Inner Music
1985
Bronze
58.4 x 23.5 x 27.9 cm
(23 x 9 1/4 x 11 in.)
The Collection of Camille O.
and William H. Cosby Jr.

plate 9

James Amos Porter
1905–1970, United States
Washerwoman
n.d.
Oil on canvas
45.8 x 33 cm (18 x 13 in.)
The Collection of Camille O.
and William H. Cosby Jr.

James Lesesne Wells
1902–1993, United States
Georgetown Garden
1958
Oil on canvas
48.3 x 55.9 cm (19 x 22 in.)
The Collection of Camille O.
and William H. Cosby Jr.

plate 11

David C. Driskell
born 1931, United States
Benin Head
c. 1978
Egg tempera on paper
19 x 19 cm (7 1/2 x 7 1/2 in.)
The Collection of Camille O.
and William H. Cosby Jr.

plate 12

Jean-Michel Basquiat
1960–1988, United States
Untitled
1981
Oil stick on buff paper
98.5 x 78 cm
(38 3/4 x 30 3/4 in.)
The Collection of Camille O.
and William H. Cosby Jr.

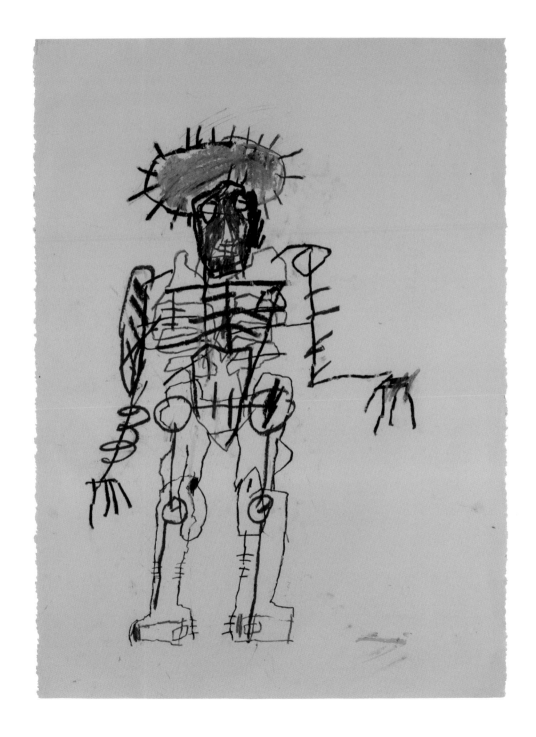

plate 13

Elizabeth Catlett
1915–2012, United States
Maternity
1980
Marble
66 x 61 x 21.6 cm
(26 x 24 x 8 1/2 in.)
The Collection of Camille O.
and William H. Cosby Jr.

A Human Presence

OR MILLENNIA THE IMAGE of the individual—the person or the self—has been a vehicle in the visual arts for both the reflection and the shaping of human identites. Researchers have found that personhood, as the concept is understood in African societies, embodies what one is as well as what one ought to be. It draws upon the human capacity to contemplate past actions and events and to perceive connections among lived experiences as part of ongoing and changing processes of identity formation.[1] Fundamental to a notion of personhood is recognizing links with others, though such relationships are not always perceived to be equal or beneficial. This recognition brings into play the concept of agency, an individual's capacity, in the words of the scholars Michael Jackson and Ivan Karp, to "actively and creatively interact with the world . . . and tackle and resolve the crises of quotidian life," even when such efforts fall short of the desired results.[2] In distinctive ways both African and African American artworks in *Conversations* employ the human figure to question ideas about personhood and agency. Art featuring the human figure often reveals how "thought is located within the body," and therefore can transform our perceptions of human experience.[3]

Consistent with art making the world over, the human figure predominates in much of Africa's arts, as artists throughout time have sought through their work to explore the human condition. In *Conversations,* works of African art dating from the seventeenth century through the twenty-first century share a human-centered approach. Both in Africa's "traditional" (or historical) works and in contemporary practice, however, depictions of men and women are not intended as literal representations of reality; they are, rather, vehicles for complex considerations of multiple realities—actual, imagined, invented, redefined, and negotiated.

Physical beauty and its opposite are frequently used in art as metaphors of important ideas and values. In much of Africa's tradition-based arts, figural sculptures often portray the human ideal as a way to communicate broader ideas about the social ideal. Such works are perceived not in isolation but as representative of wider social networks that form the fabric of human culture. In most cases of traditional African art, figural sculptures are not portraits of specific men and women, nor do they typically function as narratives of particular events. Their purposes are generally broader, necessitating a visual vocabulary of forms, symbols, and contexts capable of addressing wider social concerns. Although sweeping generalizations detract from the diversity of African cultures and their arts over time, some general observations may help to decode

fig. 48 | OVERLEAF, LEFT

[plate 33]
Charles White
1918–1979, United States
Homage to Langston Hughes
1971
Oil on canvas
122 x 122 cm (48 x 48 in.)
The Collection of Camille O.
and William H. Cosby Jr.

fig. 49 | OVERLEAF, RIGHT

[plate 26]
Bright Bimpong
born 1960, Ghana
Efo II (detail)
1993
Iron
44 x 20.6 x 20.7 cm
(17 5/16 x 8 1/8 x 8 1/8 in.)
National Museum of African
Art, Smithsonian Institution,
museum purchase, 2001-3-1

fig. 50 | OPPOSITE

[plate 14]

Lwena artist, Angola, Zambia
Female figure
Mid-20th century
Wood, pigment, antelope
horn, cloth, glass beads,
cowrie shells, metal
36.5 x 11.5 x 10.7 cm
(14 3/8 x 4 1/2 x 4 3/16 in.)
National Museum of African
Art, Smithsonian Institution,
museum purchase, 96-8-1

fig. 51 | RIGHT

[plate 15]

Baule artist, Côte d'Ivoire
Female figure
Early to mid-20th century
Wood, glass beads, gold-
alloy beads, plant fiber, white
pigment, encrustation
48.9 x 12.1 x 14.3 cm
(19 1/4 x 4 3/4 x 5 5/8 in.)
National Museum of African
Art, Smithsonian Institution,
museum purchase, 85-15-2

the visual language that African artists have employed in creating traditional works of art designed to serve local audiences at particular points in time.

In carving a human figure, a master sculptor—in Africa, traditionally male—knows precisely how to draw the viewer's eye to significant, culturally relevant details encoded in the figure's coiffure, facial features, sexual characteristics, scarification marks, attire, and jewelry. This is the case with the female figure carved by a Lwena artist. The sculpture depicts the clothing, hairstyle, and other attributes associated with female initiation and with knowledge of traditional medicine (FIG. 50, PLATE 14). Such visual markers cue ideas about gender, ethnicity, status, and achievement, along with the positive qualities associated with good character, adherence to tradition, and service to others. Indications of movement or gesture—a striding stance or hands carrying a weapon, supporting a vessel, or resting against abdomen or breasts—may convey ideas about decisiveness, leadership, initiative, nurturing, or the merits of work. Prominent sexual characteristics may reinforce the procreative roles of men and women, thus underscoring the importance of productive relationships that forge families and build communities. Representations of deities, ancestors, and other spirits rely on a familiar visual format—the body—to foster links between human potential and the abstract, extraordinary capacities and ethical teachings associated with the sacred.

Exaggerated proportions draw one's eye to those areas of the body that serve as message carriers. In certain African societies a disproportionately large head, for example, symbolizes ideas about the head as the site of self-determination, individual destiny, and intellectual and spiritual power (PLATE 20). As demonstrated in a masterfully realized female figure carved by a Baule artist, this emphasis on the head also provides ample surface for the sculptor to add culture-specific details that reflect ideas about adherence to traditional norms of beauty and decorum (FIG. 51, PLATE 15). These concepts are encoded in the figure's elaborate coiffure, scarification patterns, and refined facial features. The elongated torso provides a prominent "canvas" for the display of markers relating to gender, status, and potential. Her protruding breasts and abdomen may suggest notions of fertility and the nurturing role of women in society, whereas her rounded calves reflect Baule concepts about the social and cultural value of work and its positive contributions to family and community well-being. This figure, which depicts a spirit spouse from the other world, conceptualizes the inner beauty of a well-socialized woman through the representation of ideal physical attributes. The entire composition is beautifully balanced and reveals the hand and eye of an assured and talented artist.

The abundance of traditional African sculptures portraying a female figure with child reinforces the fundamental importance the world over of having children and raising them to be positive members of society. Carved female figures are shown nursing their children, supporting them on their laps, or carrying them on their backs—gestures that indicate the nurturing role of women and the responsibilities of motherhood (PLATE 16, PLATE 17, PLATE 18). However, the conventional interpretation of such sculptures as maternity figures may be secondary to deeper levels of meanings when the works are considered within their broader ritual or other contexts. Paired images visually reinforce notions of cooperation and collaboration, whether they are carved as separate, freestanding figures or joined together within the same composition (PLATE 19).

A mid-twentieth-century Baule male figure made for use in traditional contexts depicts changing notions of the masculine ideal through the adoption of a stylish pose and representation of Western-inspired fashionable clothing, available as part of a global circulation of people, ideas, and commodities (PLATE 21). In the contemporary realm that sense of changing individual identity within a global sphere is evident in a 1971 studio photograph of a young man taken by the Malian photographer Malick

fig. 52

[plate 22]
Malick Sidibé
born c. 1935, Mali
Untitled (detail)
1971
Black-and-white silver
gelatin photograph, glass,
cardboard, adhesive-backed
tape, ink, cord
Image: 11.9 x 8.3 cm
(4 11/16 x 3 1/4 in.)
National Museum of African
Art, Smithsonian Institution,
museum purchase, 2006-4-1

fig. 53

[plate 23]
Nontsikelelo "Lolo" Veleko
born 1977, South Africa
Kepi in Bree Street (detail)
2006
From the Beauty Is in the
Eye of the Beholder series
Digital print with pigment
dyes on cotton paper
42 x 29 cm
(16 9/16 x 11 7/16 in.)
National Museum of African
Art, Smithsonian Institution,
purchased with funds provided
by the Annie Laurie Aitken
Endowment, 2011-7-1.4

fig. 54

[plate 41]
Ethiopian artist, Orthodox
style, Ethiopia
Icon (detail)
c. 1750–1855
Distemper and gesso on
wood
34.2 x 47 x 17 cm (13 7/16 x
18 1/2 x 6 11/16 in.)
National Museum of African
Art, Smithsonian Institution,
gift of Ciro R. Taddeo, 98-3-2

Sidibé (FIG. 52, PLATE 22). Similar ideas are in play in a 2006 image by the South African photographer Nontsikelelo "Lolo" Veleko that documents innovative street fashion among South Africa's young city dwellers (FIG. 53, PLATE 23). It is part of the artist's series Beauty Is in the Eye of the Beholder, which serves to counter negative perceptions about South African urban life by presenting "sartorial success stories" about confident, positive, and stylish young people who, according to Sue Williamson, another South African artist, are "following their own creativity and casting aside all the rules."[4] The Ghanaian artist Bright Bimpong invokes long-standing conventions of the "big man"— big both in size and in accomplishment—through the voluminous tradition-inspired clothing, imposing girth, and oversized attitude of a confident, centered individual (FIG. 49, PLATE 26).

The Senegalese artist M'boz Faye and the Ethiopian artist Alexander "Skunder" Boghossian draw upon details of attire, ornamentation, and furnishings in their distinctive representations of a seated female figure (FIG. 9, PLATE 24; PLATE 25). Faye's composition is spare and charmingly naive. It stands in marked contrast to the warm, textured tones and rounded forms of Skunder's more naturalistic painting. In 1962, Skunder (the name he preferred) recalled that the work was related to a female artist who experienced extraordinary visions.[5] These are depicted, at the figure's shoulders, as oval forms, which the artist also linked to ideas of the universe and to female fertility. The structure of the composition, however, reveals the artist's familiarity with depictions of the Virgin Mary in Ethiopian liturgical art: the figure's crossed hands echo a common gesture of Mary's, and the ovals are located in the upper quadrants typically reserved for the archangels (FIGS. 54, 63, PLATE 41). These details reveal the artist's attachment to Ethiopia despite many decades of living and working outside his homeland.

Personal history and experiences of movement also inform the work of Aida

Muluneh, whose photograph *Spirit of Sisterhood* (FIG. 55, PLATE 27) explores ideas about gender and identity among young women of the Ethiopian diaspora. The work captures a sense of collaboration and mutual support as the young women determine what is hidden and what is revealed while they negotiate their individual and joint sense of identity and place in a contemporary, transnational world. As this discussion suggests, notions of tradition and modernity converge as African artists explore both continuity and change in ideas about personhood, gender, and identity in works that employ related visual vocabularies to reflect upon the past, embrace the present, and look toward the future.

Many African American artists have fashioned images of black figures that aim to depict a singular likeness, define a cultural presence, or affirm the humanity of African Americans through the index of the black body. The black figure in Western art has had a fraught and often difficult history in the hands of non-black artists who often saw black figures as one-dimensional or stereotypical. African American artists, in a conscious effort to define themselves through the redemptive power of art, created new narratives of black identities through the representation of black personhoods. Not simple portraiture, these images are explorations of multifaceted African American personas. They speak to the complexities of individual lives; they illuminate important historical figures; they celebrate self-defined beauty; and they embody the myths and traditions of black culture and the importance of family in the transmission of heritage.

As collectors, Bill and Camille Cosby have expressed a commitment to art that shows the full breadth and the dignity of the African American individual as well as the celebration of the black experience in America. Their collection embodies the multiple ways that African Americans have been engaged in the visual arts—both as artists who work in mainstream traditions such as landscape or abstraction and as artists who look

fig. 55 | OPPOSITE, TOP

[plate 27]
Aida Muluneh
born 1974, Ethiopia
Spirit of Sisterhood
2000
Cibachrome print
101.2 x 76.1 cm
(39 13/16 x 29 15/16 in.)
National Museum of African
Art, Smithsonian Institution,
museum purchase, 2004-3-1

fig. 56 | OPPOSITE, BOTTOM

[plate 28]
Joshua Johnston
c. 1765–c. 1830,
Baltimore area, Maryland
Lady on a Red Sofa (detail)
c. 1825
Oil on canvas
76.8 x 64.8 cm
(30 1/4 x 25 1/2 in.)
The Collection of Camille O.
and William H. Cosby Jr.

to represent black subjects as a cultural affirmation. From Joshua Johnston, an African American artist active in the late eighteenth and early nineteenth centuries who, by necessity, painted largely white subjects, to Charles White, whose concerns lie squarely with the narratives of African American culture in the mid-twentieth century, there is a spectrum of subjects and subjectivities represented in the Cosby collection, many of which center on the image of the body.

The oldest works in the Cosby collection are late eighteenth- and early nineteenth-century paintings by Joshua Johnston. Although there is some mystery surrounding Johnston's identity and his personal history, he is considered the first African American professional artist. Johnston gained notoriety in Baltimore, where he worked as a portrait painter from the mid-1790s to the mid-1820s. Records indicate that he was a manumitted slave who may have apprenticed with a blacksmith. He placed an advertisement for his services in a Baltimore newspaper, claiming to be a self-taught artist. Although his level of training is uncertain, traveling the road from slave to a self-promoting professional artist in the slave state of Maryland was a remarkable achievement in antebellum America.

As the world of fine-art portraiture during that era was the domain of the well-to-do, Johnston's patrons were largely white and of a high social rank. *Lady on a Red Sofa,* from about 1825, is an elegant portrait featuring a woman of style—her dress, fashionable jewels, and fine furnishings are all markers of status (FIGS. 27, 56, PLATE 28). Johnston's painterly technique is simple and flat. The background is empty and lacks depth; it is devoid of the kind of decorative embellishments that were typical of European portraits of the same period and reflects, instead, conventions in American Federalist-era painting. Portraits of American elites helped to define the young society and set it apart from European colonial traditions. Judging from the number of portraits attributed to Johnston, he was hired by a large cadre of Baltimore's art patrons. The notion that a former slave served in some small part to shape the visual identity of a newly liberated America is both ironic and inspiring. Although he painted very few African American sitters, his story is an example of the kind of unsung achievement by African Americans that the Cosbys celebrate and support in their collecting practices.

Just over one hundred years later, the African American modernist artist William Henry Johnson also pictured the beauty and elegance of the female form, but the imagery and the circumstances had drastically changed since the time of Joshua Johnston. Johnson's life and career followed the trajectory of the Great Migration of African Americans from the South to the North in the early twentieth century. Born in South Carolina, Johnson moved to New York in 1921 to attend the National Academy of Design. Seeking to further develop his talent in the center of the vibrant international modernist movement, he moved to Europe, where he was influenced by post-impressionism and expressionism. There he developed a unique style in which he explored an expressive, modernist approach to painting. Upon his return to the United States in 1938, he dedicated his artistic efforts to the representation of his own people. His *Untitled (Seated Woman)* from 1939 reflects this stage of his career and combines his expressionist style with his deepening interest in depicting black life in America. The anonymous sitter is smartly dressed and self-composed (FIGS. 8, 57, PLATE 29). Although she gazes disinterestedly back at the viewer, her red nail polish, stylish shoes, and skirt hiked above the knee reveal a subtle sass and playful sensuality. This emphasis on the urbane woman reflects the spirit of the New Negro movement and the Harlem Renaissance in which black artists exercised their own agency as creative actors to define and delimit how they were represented.

The black-consciousness era of the 1960s and 1970s ushered in a new political and cultural environment in which African American artists responded creatively and

fig. 57

[plate 29]
William Henry Johnson
1901–1970, United States
Untitled (Seated Woman)
(detail)
1939
Tempera and gouache on
paper
61 x 45.8 cm (24 x 18 in.)
The Collection of Camille O.
and William H. Cosby Jr.

fig. 58

[plate 32]
Charles White
1918–1979, United States
Seed of Heritage (detail)
1968
Ink on illustration board
152.5 x 114.3 cm
(60 x 45 in.)
The Collection of Camille O.
and William H. Cosby Jr.

assertively to the social struggles for equality in the United States. Representations of the black figure took on heightened political meaning as African American artists forged a powerful black identity in the arts. Charles White was among the most prolific and accomplished artists to poignantly and with great mastery depict both the struggles of African Americans and the great power of black heritage.

White's works revolved around the depiction of the strength and dignity of the black body from his early days as a social realist in the 1940s through his later career as one of the nation's foremost African American artists. His 1968 ink painting *Seed of Heritage* (FIGS. 35, 58, PLATE 32) shows a monumental and mythic black woman who represents the epic strength of motherhood. She is also the mythic mother of black heritage that reaches back to Africa through the African diaspora. Turning to a historical figure, White created a complex tribute to the African American poet Langston Hughes, whose poetry defined the spirit of the Harlem Renaissance. *Homage to Langston Hughes* (FIGS. 34, 48, PLATE 33) is not an actual portrait; it depicts, rather, a commanding male figure that represents the life force of one of America's most noted black cultural icons. Standing in front of a patterned backdrop, the figure is pictured as a strong presence with a seriousness of purpose. Behind him a filmstrip-like series of portraits featuring a blackface minstrel runs across the painting. The man in the portraits is reminiscent of Bert Williams, the famous African American performer who became successful as a blackface minstrel in American vaudeville, Broadway, and black music circuits in the early twentieth century—the same era in which Hughes and other African American writers and performers came to prominence. The tension between the powerful cultural figure of Langston Hughes and a black man performing "blackface" minstrelsy speaks to the struggle between stereotypical expectations and the integrity of the African American artist. Perhaps Hughes's 1925 poem "Minstrel Man" was an inspiration for White's painting. In the poem, Hughes reflects sympathetically on the emotional toll of performing blackness; his minstrel asks:

Because my mouth
Is wide with laughter,
You do not hear
My inner cry?[6]

The human figure as a powerful physical presence is also embodied in the many sculptures by Elizabeth Catlett in the Cosby collection. The Cosbys shared a close relationship with the expatriate African American artist, who spent much of her career living in Mexico. Her art is socially conscious and dedicated to depicting the struggles and triumphs of African Americans in their quest for equality. Her visual language is infused with traditional African and pre-Columbian forms. Admiring Catlett's depictions of strong and beautiful black women, and her masterful use of natural materials, the Cosbys commissioned the mahogany sculpture *Woman Resting* (FIG. 59, PLATE 35) and the marble sculpture *Maternity* (SEE PLATE 13). The works celebrate the eternal female form and the universal essence of motherhood. The Cosbys commissioned *The Family* in a tribute to their own family; the nearly life-size marble sculpture features a mother and a father figure in an embrace, with profiles of children incised on the side of the work (FIG. 36, PLATE 34). The personal importance of family to the collectors cannot be overstated, but the critical mass of images of family and maternity in their collection speaks to the larger importance of family in the maintenance and transmission of African American culture.

In keeping with the Cosbys' interest in family, many of the images in their collection depict black youth. The New York sculptor Augusta Savage's 1929 *Gamin* (PLATE 37) is a small and poignant rendering of a Harlem boy. This warm interpretation of an

fig. 59

[plate 35]
Elizabeth Catlett
1915–2012, United States
Woman Resting (detail)
1981
Mahogany, paint
49.8 x 44.5 x 34.3 cm
(19 5/8 x 17 1/2 x 13 1/2 in.)
The Collection of Camille O.
and William H. Cosby Jr.

anonymous street urchin reminds us of the uncertain plight of children during the Great Depression. In Paris that same year, Archibald J. Motley Jr. painted *Senegalese Boy* (FIG. 60, PLATE 38). Motley was a Chicago painter who, like many American artists in the 1920s, went to Paris to study art. At the time of Motley's sojourn, Senegal was a French colony and Paris was home to a large community of people from the African continent. A number of Motley's Parisian cabaret scenes from the 1920s depict black people from across the diaspora who came together in celebration of jazz music. Motley's depiction of the Senegalese youth—his rich skin tone, striking features, fashionable attire, and quiet reserve—is one of his many works that bear witness to the interconnected experiences of African diapsoric peoples.

NOTES

1. For concepts of personhood and identity in African cultures, see Jackson and Karp 1990, 16, drawing on the work of Marcel Mauss and Meyer Fortes. See also Kaphagawani 1998, 169; Holdstock 2000, 89.

2. Jackson and Karp 1990, 16.

3. Ibid., 17.

4. Williamson 2009, 300.

5. *Skunder Boghossian* 1962.

6. Langston Hughes, "Minstrel Man," in Hughes 1995, 61. See Barnwell 2002 for an in-depth discussion of the work of Charles White.

plate 14
_____

Lwena artist, Angola, Zambia
Female figure
Mid-20th century
Wood, pigment, antelope
horn, cloth, glass beads,
cowrie shells, metal
36.5 x 11.5 x 10.7 cm
(14 3/8 x 4 1/2 x 4 3/16 in.)
National Museum of African
Art, Smithsonian Institution,
museum purchase, 96-8-1

plate 17

Kongo artist, Mayombe
region, Democratic Republic
of the Congo
Female figure with child
Late 19th to early 20th
century
Wood, metal, brass tacks,
resin, pigment
24.4 x 9.2 x 8.9 cm
(9 5/8 x 3 5/8 x 3 1/2 in.)
National Museum of African
Art, Smithsonian Institution,
museum purchase, 86-12-12

Asante artist, Ghana
Female figure with child
Late 19th to mid-20th
century
Wood, pigment, glass beads,
fiber, nails
56.5 x 15.7 x 24.5 cm
(22 1/4 x 6 3/16 x 9 5/8 in.)
National Museum of African
Art, Smithsonian Institution,
gift of Mr. and Mrs. Arnold J.
Alderman, 2001-22-1

plate 19

Senufo artist, Côte d'Ivoire
Male and female figures
Mid-20th century
Wood
Male: 146.1 x 29.2 x 22.9 cm
(57 1/2 x 11 1/2 x 9 in.)
Female: 114.3 x 25.4 x
22.9 cm (45 x 10 x 9 in.)
National Museum of African
Art, Smithsonian Institution,
gift of Samuel Rubin, 78-14-7
and 78-14-8

Fang artist, Gabon
Reliquary guardian head
Late 19th to early 20th
century
Wood, metal, oil patina
39.5 x 14 x 8.5 cm
(15 9/16 x 5 1/2 x 3 3/8 in.)
National Museum of African
Art, Smithsonian Institution,
gift of Walt Disney World
Co., a subsidiary of The Walt
Disney Company, 2005-6-98

plate 23

Nontsikelelo "Lolo" Veleko
born 1977, South Africa
Kepi in Bree Street
2006
From the Beauty Is in the
Eye of the Beholder series
Digital print with pigment
dyes on cotton paper
42 x 29 cm
(16 9/16 x 11 7/16 in.)
National Museum of African
Art, Smithsonian Institution,
purchased with funds pro-
vided by the Annie Laurie
Aitken Endowment,
2011-7-1.4

plate 24

M'boz Faye
n.d., Senegal
Untitled
1970
Paint on burlap
66.8 x 56.9 x 4.4 cm
(26 5/16 x 22 3/8 x 1 3/4 in.)
National Museum of African
Art, Smithsonian Institution,
gift of Samella Lewis,
2010-14-18

plate 25

Alexander "Skunder"
Boghossian
1937–2003, Ethiopia
Hallucination
1961
Oil on canvas
99 x 63.6 cm (39 x 25 1/16 in.)
National Museum of African
Art, Smithsonian Institution,
gift of Merton Simpson in
memory of Sylvia H.
Williams, 96-14-1

plate 26 | LEFT

Bright Bimpong
born 1960, Ghana
Efo II
1993
Iron
44 x 20.6 x 20.7 cm
(17 5/16 x 8 1/8 x 8 1/8 in.)
National Museum of African
Art, Smithsonian Institution,
museum purchase, 2001-3-1

plate 27 | OPPOSITE

Aida Muluneh
born 1974, Ethiopia
Spirit of Sisterhood
2000
Cibachrome print
101.2 x 76.1 cm
(39 13/16 x 29 15/16 in.)
National Museum of African
Art, Smithsonian Institution,
museum purchase, 2004-3-1

plate 28

Joshua Johnston
c. 1765–c. 1830,
Baltimore area, Maryland
Lady on a Red Sofa
c. 1825
Oil on canvas
76.8 x 64.8 cm
(30 1/4 x 25 1/2 in.)
The Collection of Camille O.
and William H. Cosby Jr.

plate 29

William Henry Johnson
1901–1970, United States
Untitled (Seated Woman)
1939
Tempera and gouache on
paper
61 x 45.8 cm (24 x 18 in.)
The Collection of Camille O.
and William H. Cosby Jr.

plate 30 | LEFT

Charles Alston
1907–1977, United States
Woman and Child
c. 1955
Oil on canvas
127 x 91.5 cm (50 x 36 in.)
The Collection of Camille O.
and William H. Cosby Jr.

plate 31 | OPPOSITE

Mary Lovelace O'Neal
born 1942, United States
From the Desert Women
series
1991
Monoprint
70.3 x 100 cm
(27 5/8 x 39 3/8 in.)
The Collection of Camille O.
and William H. Cosby Jr.

plate 32

Charles White
1918–1979, United States
Seed of Heritage
1968
Ink on illustration board
152.5 x 114.3 cm
(60 x 45 in.)
The Collection of Camille O.
and William H. Cosby Jr.

plate 33

Charles White
1918–1979, United States
Homage to Langston Hughes
1971
Oil on canvas
122 x 122 cm (48 x 48 in.)
The Collection of Camille O.
and William H. Cosby Jr.

Elizabeth Catlett
1915–2012, United States
Woman Resting
1981
Mahogany, paint
49.8 x 44.5 x 34.3 cm
(19 5/8 x 17 1/2 x 13 1/2 in.)
The Collection of Camille O.
and William H. Cosby Jr.

Spiritualities

N CONVERSATIONS, selected works of African and African American art provide opportunities to examine the intentions and motivations of artists who creatively explore multiple understandings of the spiritual. The artworks considered in this section span continents, reflecting both long-standing traditions and responses to new sources of inspiration. They suggest the diverse ways in which artists engage spiritual and religious subject matter as strategies to address current ideas and issues. What emerges is not a unified narrative on an exceedingly complex topic but, rather, selected illustrations of the importance of spiritual beliefs and practices in African and African American communities and the means by which these have been translated into the visual arts.

The diversity of religions in Africa reflects the continent's long history—a topic well beyond the scope of this book. Suffice it to say that traditional religions were and continue to be relevant to many urban and rural Africans, who may honor ancestral and other spirits or worship multiple deities alongside a single creator god while at the same time embracing the tenets of Christian, Islamic, or other religious practice. Multiple spiritual pathways are options to be accessed in the pursuit of a moral life.

Religious thought the world over has tended to ponder the creation of the cosmos and the role of humans in it. Over time, African communities developed worldviews that were articulated through myth, oral history, and religious beliefs and practices, and in some cases visualized through cosmological models that imaged ideal conceptions of the world. For example, a figurative stool made by a Dogon artist from Mali, possibly in the late nineteenth or early twentieth century, has been interpreted as representing the Dogon myth of the founding of the world and the creation of humankind (FIG. 62, PLATE 39). In both Dogon myth and Dogon art, paired figures with upraised arms recall the founding ancestral spirits, or *nommo,* who descended from their home in the sky to the terrain below, their journey thus linking the two domains—sky and earth—represented by the stool's dual disks.

Art historian Karen E. Milbourne summarizes beautifully how earth "has been invoked to powerful effect across diverse African populations as a binder for potent medicines, as a source of intrinsic force and power, as a home to the sacred, and as a medium through which to express poignant messages of place, identity, and gender."[1] Such ideas informed the creation of power objects in the nineteenth and early to mid-twentieth centuries among a range of central African groups, including the Kongo, Songye, Suku, Yaka, Yombe, and Vili.

fig. 61 | OVERLEAF, LEFT

[plate 51]
William Henry Johnson
1901–1970, United States
Ezekiel Saw the Wheel
c. 1939
Gouache and silkscreen
on paper
44.5 x 29.3 cm
(17 1/2 x 11 1/2 in.)
The Collection of Camille O.
and William H. Cosby Jr.

fig. 62 | OVERLEAF, RIGHT

[plate 39]
Dogon artist, Mali
Stool
Possibly late 19th to early
20th century
Wood, pigment
36.5 x 32.8 x 31.8 cm
(14 3/8 x 12 15/16 x 12 1/2 in.)
National Museum of African
Art, Smithsonian Institution,
gift of Walt Disney World Co.,
a subsidiary of The Walt
Disney Company, 2005-6-40

For the Kongo, a power figure, or *nkisi nkondi,* served as the physical container for a spirit from the other world, the land of the dead (PLATE 40). For the sculpture to be effective in its mission to heal, protect, or punish, it required activation by a ritual specialist, or *nganga,* an individual with specialized knowledge of traditional medicines, including earthen materials. Powerful ingredients were attached to the figure or inserted into cavities located at especially potent sites, such as the top of the head, the back, and/or the abdomen. The cavity was sealed with resin and at times with a mirror—its reflective qualities were meant to deflect attacks from potentially dangerous external sources. Once the figure was thus armed, the ritual specialist would attract the figure's attention by exploding gunpowder in front of it and through invocations and music.

Selected works of art introduce some of the ways in which African artists created objects designed to communicate spiritual concepts to specific local or regional communities at particular points in time. Ethiopia, for example, is noted for the production of exquisite liturgical arts that reflect the nation's embrace of Orthodox Christianity in approximately the fourth century. Beautifully crafted processional, handheld, and pendant crosses fashioned of silver and brass, illustrated prayer books, healing scrolls, and icons were embellished with images of Jesus, the Virgin Mary, saints, and at times the patrons who commissioned the objects. They were often identified by inscriptions in *ge'ez,* the liturgical language of the Ethiopian church, which also enhanced the healing, protective, and devotional qualities of these artworks. Devotion to the Virgin Mary was and remains extremely popular in Ethiopia, evinced by the

fig. 63

[plate 41]
Ethiopian artist, Orthodox style, Ethiopia
Icon
c. 1750–1855
Distemper and gesso on wood
34.2 x 47 x 17 cm
(13 7/16 x 18 1/2 x 6 11/16 in.)
National Museum of African Art, Smithsonian Institution, gift of Ciro R. Taddeo, 98-3-2

sheer number of religious art forms that bear her image, such as an exquisitely painted icon dating from the mid-eighteenth to the mid-nineteenth century (FIGS. 54, 63, PLATE 41). The format of the icon is fairly standard: a central figure of Mary holding the Christ Child, with side panels depicting the Crucifixion, the apostles or saints, Saint George slaying the dragon, and Christ raising Adam and Eve. The green and deep blue hues of the composition are typical of the time period, while the influence in Ethiopia of a Western early medieval painting of the Virgin (from the church of Santa Maria Maggiore, Rome) is reflected in Mary's crossed hands, the decorative folds and motifs of her shawl, and the inclusion of a book in the hands of the Christ Child. Of particular interest in this icon is the handkerchief that Mary holds.[2]

Christianity's introduction to central Africa dates to 1483, with the arrival of the Portuguese along the coast of the Kongo kingdom (located in the north of modern Angola and the south of the present-day Democratic Republic of the Congo), which was well established by then. A Christian presence existed there until the mid-eighteenth century, but the extent to which the Kongo peoples absorbed Christian rites and materials into their own practices varied. Indeed, Christianity did not supplant local beliefs but was adopted by Kongo rulers as a strategy to strengthen trade and political relations with foreign powers. Scepters, staffs, and crucifixes were used as local symbols of status and prestige devoid of specific Christian interpretations. Long after the missionary efforts waned in the mid-eighteenth century, Kongo artists continued creating crucifixes with images of Christ that tended to have African features (FIG. 7, PLATE 43; FIG. 64, PLATE 42). This practice likely reflected the local relevance of the cruciform itself, for the cross in Kongo cosmology is a *dikenga,* or graphic sign, that represents the meeting of this world and the spirit world.

fig. 64 | LEFT

[plate 42]
Kongo artist, Democratic Republic of the Congo, Republic of the Congo
Crucifix
Late 17th to early 18th century
Copper alloy
33.3 x 14.9 x 2.9 cm
(13 1/8 x 5 7/8 x 1 1/8 in.)
National Museum of African Art, Smithsonian Institution, gift of Ernst Anspach, 91-10-1

fig. 65 | OPPOSITE

[plate 44]
Ezrom Legae
1938–1999, South Africa
Sacrifice
1991
Bronze
84.4 x 45 x 26.4 cm
(33 1/4 x 17 11/16 x 10 3/8 in.)
National Museum of African Art, Smithsonian Institution, museum purchase, 98-25-1

The arts of Africa include numerous other examples of the ways in which Africans respond to imported ideas and images. For example, depictions of Mami Wata (Mother Water), a powerful water spirit recognized by peoples throughout Africa, draw on a nineteenth-century lithograph of a female snake charmer that was made in Hamburg, Germany.[3] In the 1950s this image, reprinted in a calendar issued by an Indian company, was circulated widely in western and central Africa. The woman's exotic, foreign appearance, her long, flowing hair, and her mastery over serpents captured public attention and blended with earlier, local ideas of water spirits and deities that were associated with fertility, power, and wealth achieved in part through river and coastal trade. Devotion to Mami Wata within and outside Africa is reflected in masks and figures that bear her image, including a brightly hued carving by an Anang artist from southeastern Nigeria that conceptualizes all the exotic attributes found in the German lithograph (PLATE 45). Mami Wata's popularity extends to the African diaspora, where altars display her image alongside offerings of the beautiful, exotic, and imported prestige goods that she prefers.

In the contemporary sphere, oblique references to spiritual concepts sometimes stand for much more. For example, the brutality, poverty, and injustices that mounted in South Africa during apartheid were critiqued by the artist Ezrom Legae in compelling sculptural works that depict injured or dead animals in contorted postures. The artist grew up in Soweto and studied at the Polly Street Art Centre in Johannesburg, the first public art school open to black students. His bronze sculpture *Sacrifice* reconfigures the pathos of Michelangelo's *Pietà*—the mother of Christ holding her dead son—by depicting a woman holding a dead goat (FIG. 65, PLATE 44). Although the goat recalls the practice of animal ritual sacrifice in Africa, for the artist it serves as a metaphor of the fate of black activists who struggled, and continue to struggle, against acts of violence and injustice perpetrated against South African people of color during apartheid and in the post-apartheid years. Through the use of difficult and brutal imagery, the artist cries out for social justice and for peace—something that can be achieved in South Africa only by an end to long-standing racial divisions and the poverty they engender.

The internal struggle involved in that search for peace is powerfully realized in *Boy and the Candle* by Gerard Sekoto, a pioneer of African modernism who was among the first black South African artists to work with oil paints (FIG. 66, PLATE 46). In this delicately hued work, the artist reveals his command of light and shadow to illuminate the subject in a soft, warm glow. The boy's face, however, seems prematurely aged, rendered with taut skin over prominent cheekbones, deep eye sockets, heavy eyes, and a pensive expression on the pursed lips. Although the paint-ing depicts a quiet, contemplative moment, it is hard to shake the feeling that this peaceful scene is informed by a weary suffering. Indeed, although the artist enjoyed a measure of recognition and patronage, Sekoto suffered under South Africa's system of racial segregation and eventually relocated in 1947 to Paris, where he lived out his days in self-exile. Something of that lifetime of struggle is intimated in *Boy and the Candle.*

A similar quality of light infuses Henry Ossawa Tanner's *The Thankful Poor* (FIG. 67, PLATE 47), in which an elderly man and a young boy sit in prayer at a humble dinner table. Bathed in soft, glowing light, this view of an intimate moment between black

fig. 66 | LEFT

[plate 46]
Gerard Sekoto
1913–1993, South Africa
Boy and the Candle
1943
Oil on canvas
46.2 x 36 cm
(18 3/16 x 13 1/4 in.)
National Museum of African Art, Smithsonian Institution, museum purchase, 2000-3-1

fig. 67 | OPPOSITE

[plate 47]
Henry Ossawa Tanner
1859–1937, United States
The Thankful Poor
1894
Oil on canvas
90.3 x 112.5 cm
(35 1/2 x 44 1/4 in.)
The Collection of Camille O. and William H. Cosby Jr.

family members practicing the daily ritual of prayer and thankfulness is a milestone in the history of African American art. The first modern African American artist to gain renown in both America and Europe, Tanner was one of the earliest to offer a counternarrative to the prevailing stereotypes of African Americans. Painted in 1894, *The Thankful Poor* offers a dignified view of African American spiritual practice in a direct response to the comic and degrading images of black people that dominated turn-of-the-century visual culture. Both *The Thankful Poor* and Tanner's *The Banjo Lesson* (1893; Hampton University Museum) are in keeping with genre paintings of the era by the well-known American artists Thomas Eakins and Thomas Hovenden. Yet Tanner's images are remarkable because they were offered by a black artist whose intention was to use the language of American and European painting to present a more serious and sympathetic vision of African American life.

Tanner's scene of prayer at a simple table depicts black religious practice in the most human terms. At the core of Tanner's *The Thankful Poor* is the centrality of religiosity and spirituality in African American life, and the painting reflects the artist's deep commitment to religious subject matter. The work revolves around the intergenerational bonds between an older black man and a younger boy, and it speaks to the importance of familial relationships and the transmission and preservation of black Christian culture. As timely as this material was during the rise of a new black consciousness at the close of the nineteenth century, Tanner did not continue to address themes of black culture. Instead, during Tanner's long career as an expatriate artist living in Paris, he gained his international reputation as a painter of biblical themes such as *The Good Shepherd* (FIG. 68, PLATE 48). He was held up as an exemplar of "Negro" achievement by the African American intelligentsia, but he was also criticized by some for not devoting more of his creative energies and position in the art world to representing "Negro" life.[4] In an era when W. E. B. Du Bois and Alain LeRoy Locke were crafting a New Negro movement in which visual culture played a major role in affirming the humanity of African Americans, it was disappointing to many that Tanner was not actively engaged in the politics of race and representation. *The Thankful Poor* was Tanner's last canvas dedicated to African American life, making it highly significant in the history of African American art. Although the Cosbys own several works by Tanner, their acquisition at auction of *The Thankful Poor,* an important part of African American cultural patrimony that had been virtually lost for decades, is one of their major achievements as collectors.[5]

The notion that black people could visually embody the stories of Christianity came to the fore during the Harlem Renaissance, when some African American artists took a radical turn by depicting biblical narratives using the black figure. In *Crucifixion* (FIG. 25, PLATE 50), Aaron Douglas, the illustrator and painter whose modernist aesthetic defined the "Negro" idiom of the Harlem Renaissance, foregrounds the North African biblical character Simon of Cyrene in his image of a scene that usually focused on Christ. Douglas's 1934 painting is based on one of his illustrations for James Weldon Johnson's *God's Trombones* (1927), a book of sermons in verse that took their inspiration from what Johnson referred to as the "old-time Negro preacher."[6] Steeped in black modes of Christianity, *Crucifixion* privileges the contribution of the African Simon of Cyrene as he carries the cross for Christ on his way to be crucified. Fashioned in Douglas's signature style, Simon's face is masklike in profile, with the full, contrasting lips suggesting black physiognomy. A haloed Christ is pictured as one of the smaller figures in the procession

fig. 68 | OPPOSITE, TOP

[plate 48]

Henry Ossawa Tanner

1859–1937, United States

The Good Shepherd (detail)

1920s

Oil on canvas

64.8 x 81.3 cm (25 1/2 x 32 in.)

The Collection of Camille O.
and William H. Cosby Jr.

fig. 69 | OPPOSITE, BOTTOM

[plate 49]

Horace Pippin

1888–1946, United States

The Holy Mountain I (detail)

1944

Oil on canvas

76.2 x 91.5 cm (30 x 36 in.)

The Collection of Camille O.
and William H. Cosby Jr.

to Calvary. Douglas's visual language combines the African ancestral legacy with a contemporary modernist aesthetic sensibility and applies it to a traditional black Christian theme, synthesizing old and new in the artist's own brand of African American modernism.

Although a sense of spiritual connectedness permeates the work of African American artists, their approaches to Christianity, religiosity, and spirituality are largely personal and highly distinctive. *The Holy Mountain I* (FIGS. 32, 69, PLATE 49) is Horace Pippin's vision of the Peaceable Kingdom, from Isaiah's biblical prophecy, wherein animals of all varieties coexist harmoniously with humans. Pippin's black shepherd signifies the Good Shepherd, the Old Testament image that prefigures Christ. In the background among the dense trees, cruciform grave markers and soldiers threaten the idyllic scene and seem incongruous in this homage to the ideal peace. The reference to war and death is certainly autobiographical, as Pippin sustained injuries during his military service in World War I. Vacillating between biblical prophecy and the trauma of war in the early twentieth century, Pippin's vision is an idiosyncratic one.[7]

Minnie Evans's *Design Made at Airlie Garden* (FIGS. 31, 70, PLATE 52) similarly presents a highly personal image of the spiritual realm. Evans was a visionary artist who operated outside the traditional arenas of professional art making. A domestic worker and gatekeeper at Airlie Gardens in Wilmington, North Carolina, Evans began to create art late in life as a response to a message from God. She was deeply religious and crafted her own visual language of mythic figures that exist in a magical space animated by motifs from the natural world.

The printmaker Margo Humphrey was profoundly inspired by the freedom of expression—the freedom from constraints of traditional religious and social doctrine—that she saw in the work of self-taught and visionary artists. Humphrey herself earned a master's degree from Stanford University and had professional training in printmaking, yet her work was emboldened by that of highly imaginative outsider artists such as Minnie Evans and Sister Gertrude Morgan. In *The Last Bar-B-Que* (FIGS. 33, 71, PLATE 53), Humphrey refashions Leonardo da Vinci's *The Last Supper* into a self-assured and colorful vision of humanity gathering around the table of peace. The kaleidoscopic disciples—blue, brown, and yellow; male and female—represent an amalgam of religions, races, and cultural traditions that transcends time and space. Set in Fiji, where Humphrey spent a summer teaching, the scene shows the group dining on tropical fruits, wine, bread, and of course barbecued chicken and watermelon. For Humphrey, this spiritual and multicultural feast elevated the foods that were once used to denigrate African Americans. Humphrey's exuberant and boundary-breaking approach to this Christian theme combines irreverence, irony, respect, and a healthy dose of humor.[8]

In African American culture, Christianity is a foundational force that is central to narratives of redemption and salvation dating back to slavery. Although expressed with multiple interpretive strategies and visual languages, artistic representation of Christianity in terms of black figures and black imagery was important for demonstrating ownership and true investment in this spiritual tradition. The same can be said about African representations of Christianity and the development of syncretic faith traditions, some of which have transformed beliefs and imagery associated with particular Christian saints into "Africanized" motifs and religious concepts addressing specifically local concerns.

In African and African American contexts, works of art are powerful vehicles for exploring the universal desire to understand the world and one's place in it. That quest is often couched in terms of history, myth, and religious beliefs and practices that offer touchstones to guide one along a moral path. Art plays a role in showing a way forward, in illustrating the critical importance of being part of something larger, and in forging

fig. 70

[plate 52]
Minnie Evans
1892–1987, United States
Design Made at Airlie Garden (detail)
1969
Oil and mixed media on canvas board
41.3 x 57.8 cm
(16 1/4 x 22 3/4 in.)
The Collection of Camille O. and William H. Cosby Jr.

connections to others in ways that reinforce—and insist on—the recognition of a common humanity.

NOTES

1. Milbourne 2013, 53.

2. Heldman 1993, 75, catalogue entries page 100 and page 245. The image of the Virgin from the Church of Santa Maria Maggiore in Rome may have reached Ethiopia through prints disseminated by Jesuit missionaries in the sixteenth and seventeenth centuries. Heldman notes that the handkerchief refers to an account of the miraculous appearance of Mary in the cupola of the church of Dabra Metmaq in Ethiopia. The story has it that Mary took in her hand a handkerchief that had been thrown into the cupola by one of the faithful.

3. For more information on the origins of the snake-charmer imagery associated with Mami Wata, see Drewal 2008, 50–52.

4. Childs 2012, 102. For additional discussion of the work of Henry Ossawa Tanner, see Powell 2012.

5. See David C. Driskell's recollections of the Cosbys' acquisition of *The Thankful Poor* in the preface and "Perspectives of an Artist and a Curator: A Conversation with David C. Driskell," this volume.

6. Johnson 1927, 2, 38 (Douglas's drawing of the Crucifixion).

7. For more on the work of Horace Pippin, see Roberts 1999.

8. See Childs 2009 for additional discussion of the work of Margo Humphrey.

fig. 71

[plate 53]
Margo Humphrey
born 1942, United States
The Last Bar-B-Que
1988
Lithograph
66 x 96.5 cm (26 x 38 in.)
The Collection of Camille O.
and William H. Cosby Jr.

plate 39

Dogon artist, Mali
Stool
Possibly late 19th to early
20th century
Wood, pigment
36.5 x 32.8 x 31.8 cm
(14 3/8 x 12 15/16 x 12 1/2 in.)
National Museum of African
Art, Smithsonian Institution,
gift of Walt Disney World Co.,
a subsidiary of The Walt
Disney Company, 2005-6-40

Kongo artist, Democratic
Republic of the Congo
Male figure *(nkisi nkondi)*
Late 19th to mid-20th
century
Wood, glass, iron, pigment,
cloth, plant fiber, horn, nails
42.7 x 26.6 x 19.3 cm
(16 13/16 x 10 1/2 x 7 5/8 in.)
National Museum of African
Art, Smithsonian Institution,
gift of Dr. and Mrs. Robert
Kuhn, 91-22-1

plate 41

Ethiopian artist, Orthodox
style, Ethiopia
Icon
c. 1750–1855
Distemper and gesso on
wood
34.2 x 47 x 17 cm
(13 7/16 x 18 1/2 x 6 11/16 in.)
National Museum of African
Art, Smithsonian Institution,
gift of Ciro R. Taddeo, 98-3-2

plate 44

Ezrom Legae
1938–1999, South Africa
Sacrifice
1991
Bronze
84.4 x 45 x 26.4 cm
(33 1/4 x 17 11/16 x 10 3/8 in.)
National Museum of African
Art, Smithsonian Institution,
museum purchase, 98-25-1

plate 45

Anang artist, Nigeria
Mami Wata figure
Late 20th century
Wood, paint, raffia
67.5 x 53 x 28 cm
(26 9/16 x 20 7/8 x 11 in.)
National Museum of African
Art, Smithsonian Institution,
gift of Flora Edouwaye S.
Kaplan, 2009-16-1

plate 48

Henry Ossawa Tanner
1859–1937, United States
The Good Shepherd
1920s
Oil on canvas
64.8 x 81.3 cm (25 1/2 x 32 in.)
The Collection of Camille O.
and William H. Cosby Jr.

plate 49

Horace Pippin
1888–1946, United States
The Holy Mountain I
1944
Oil on canvas
76.2 x 91.5 cm (30 x 36 in.)
The Collection of Camille O.
and William H. Cosby Jr.

plate 50

Aaron Douglas
1899–1979, United States
Crucifixion
1934
Oil on Masonite
122 x 91.5 cm (48 x 36 in.)
The Collection of Camille O.
and William H. Cosby Jr.

plate 51

William Henry Johnson
1901–1970, United States
Ezekiel Saw the Wheel
c. 1939
Gouache and silkscreen
on paper
44.5 x 29.3 cm
(17 1/2 x 11 1/2 in.)
The Collection of Camille O.
and William H. Cosby Jr.

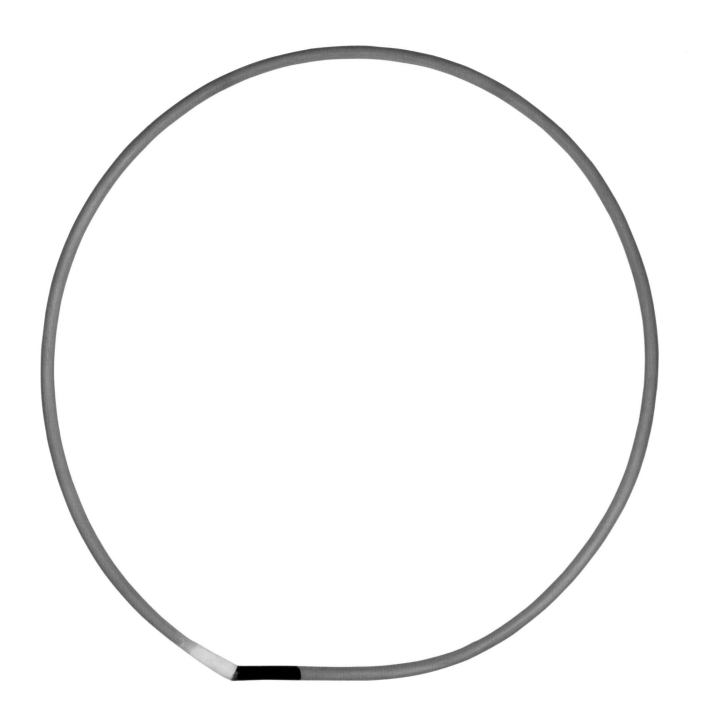

plate 54

Martin Puryear
born 1941, United States
Nexus
1979
Stained, ebonized, and
gessoed yellow cedar
Diam: 114.3 cm (45 in.)
W: 3.81 cm (1 1/2 in.)
The Collection of Camille O.
and William H. Cosby Jr.

GODFRIED K.A. — — — TION OF A S — — HIP. DONKOR 92

Power and Politics

AFRICAN AND AFRICAN AMERICAN artists in *Conversations* employ a range of visual strategies—upended figures; blood seeping from wounds; poses and gestures denoting individual or collective strength, or its absence—in their explorations of power and its social and political implications. Power, authority, and ideology are interrelated and involve more than a simple struggle between dominant and subordinate positions.[1] Power is also dynamic, creative, and enabling, embodying human agency that engages with and contests expressions of power and authority through ideology and practice, including appropriation, resistance, transformation, and the formation—or just the hope—of a new order.

Works of art are powerful mechanisms for conveying meaning. Their potency partially derives from the emotional and intellectual intensity that accompanies one's encounters with objects, an intensity that is influenced by aesthetic, experiential, and other factors. *Conversations* brings together a remarkable group of artworks that examine power from distinct points of view. In most works in this section, the human figure is evident or at least implied, underscoring the role that human agency plays in articulations of power.

Human control over unruly, unpredictable forces, for example, unites three very different sculptures dating from the early twentieth century—one by an African American artist, and two by African artists. The former was created with the international fine-art market in mind; the latter served locally specific audiences and contexts. All three draw on the idiom of a human figure astride an animal as a way to explore ideas about power.

In Africa's traditional arts, ferocious, fantastic, and composite depictions often serve as counterpoints to positive ideals by visualizing the opposite—negative, antisocial qualities that should be avoided. A Pende artist from the Democratic Republic of the Congo considered this concept in depicting a man riding a buffalo (FIG. 75, PLATE 55), an animal associated with the volatile and dangerous forces of the bush or wilderness— the area beyond the cultured, cultivated world of humans. The rider's peaked headdress denotes an individual of considerable authority and high status, likely a ruler, whose capacity to tame the dangerous forest buffalo illustrates the authority he exerts over both man and nature. Along similar lines, an Isoko artist from Nigeria created a sculpture known as *ivri,* conceptualized as a composite creature that blends human and animal characteristics along with elements of an extraordinary creature that defies precise identification (FIG. 74, PLATE 56). The contrasts visually establish an unfamiliar and potentially dangerous and powerful realm well beyond settled community life and ordi-

fig. 72 | OVERLEAF, LEFT

[plate 58]
Godfried Donkor
born 1964, Ghana
From Slave to Champ I
(detail)
1992
Mixed media on paper
62.7 x 47.5 cm
(24 11/16 x 18 11/16 in.)
National Museum of African
Art, Smithsonian Institution,
purchased with funds provided by the Smithsonian
Collections Acquisition
Program, 96-21-2

fig. 73 | OVERLEAF, RIGHT

[plate 70]
Eldzier Cortor
born 1916, United States
Still Life: Souvenir No. IV
(detail)
1982
Oil on canvas
144.8 x 83.8 cm (57 x 33 in.)
The Collection of Camille O.
and William H. Cosby Jr.

fig. 74 | OPPOSITE

[plate 56]
Isoko artist, Nigeria
Figure *(ivri)*
Late 19th to mid-20th
century
Wood
66 x 14.5 x 16.5 cm
(26 x 5 11/16 x 6 1/2 in.)
National Museum of African
Art, Smithsonian Institution,
gift of Walt Disney World Co.,
a subsidiary of The Walt
Disney Company, 2005-6-122

fig. 75 | RIGHT

[plate 55]
Pende artist, Democratic
Republic of the Congo
Man riding a buffalo
Early 20th century
Wood, pigment, brass tacks
56.5 x 23 x 32.5 cm
(22 1/4 x 9 1/16 x 12 13/16 in.)
National Museum of African
Art, Smithsonian Institution,
estate of Barbara and Joseph
Goldenberg, 2011-4-1

nary human abilities. At the time *ivri* carvings were made and used, they served to recognize human accomplishments, but they also sought to tame forceful personality traits or to channel them into appropriate behavior. This idea is conveyed by the ferocious-looking animal with gaping maw that is subdued by the powerful male figure astride it. Such objects illustrate how anomalous creatures as well as recognizable animals can be called upon—through visually compelling works of art—to exemplify moral teachings, and thus to enter into beneficial relationships with humans.

In the sculpture entitled *Peace Halting the Ruthlessness of War,* the African American artist Meta Vaux Warwick Fuller convincingly evokes the mythic battle waged to secure peace in the face of war (FIG. 4, PLATE 66). War is depicted as a powerful equestrian figure straining at the reins, as a horse tramples the unfortunate, who writhe in anguish beneath its feet and seek mercy. The sculpture originally included a figure of Peace in the form of an angel, but it was later removed by the artist.[2] Fuller, a Boston-based sculptor, was a community activist committed to both suffragist causes and the peace movement that arose at the start of World War I. Studying in Paris at the end of the nineteenth century, Fuller had visited the studio of Auguste Rodin and had been deeply moved by his work. *Peace Halting the Ruthlessness of War* reflects the influence of Rodin's powerfully expressive handling of materials and emphasis on human drama. Although the sculpture was never cast in Fuller's lifetime, the plaster sketch of this emotional response to the horrors of the Great War was a prizewinner in the local Women's Peace Party art contest in 1917.[3] In 1998 the Cosbys had the original wax model cast in bronze for the first time, recovering and preserving this important work by Fuller.

Indications of movement or gesture—a striding stance; hands raised to block, defend, or comfort; groups leaning together to commiserate—can communicate decisiveness, leadership, or a call to action. The Senegalese artist Ousmane Sow addresses the legacies of slavery and colonialism in his monumental sculpture depicting Toussaint Louverture (1743–1803), the leader of the Haitian revolution that liberated the island and the enslaved Africans there from French colonial control. The artist effectively conveys Toussaint's determination and recognition of the challenges ahead by the figure's commanding presence, powerful stance, well-defined musculature, and steely gaze (FIG. 1, PLATE 57). These qualities of physical and emotional power are counterbalanced by Toussaint's compassion as he extends a hand to the enslaved woman suffering at his feet. The subject matter was selected by the artist in response to the government of France's call to artists from its former colonies to create works of art in celebration of the bicentennial of the French Revolution in 1989. The sculpture is a tour-de-force statement about the universal struggle for freedom and equality, and it effectively demonstrates how African artists are engaged, through their practice, in wider, global concerns.

Both the Ghanaian artist Godfried Donkor's *From Slave to Champ I* (FIG. 72, PLATE 58) and the African American artist Eldzier Cortor's *Still Life: Souvenir No. IV* (FIG. 73, PLATE 70) employ well-known images of Jack Johnson, the first African American heavyweight champion, adopting the stance—feet wide apart, arms raised, fists clenched—of a boxer prepared to do battle in the ring. Johnson was a flamboyant and controversial boxer who defeated a series of white contenders seeking to gain the title he held from 1908 to 1915. In distinctive ways both works examine issues of race and economic inequality as legacies of enslavement. In Donkor's work, Johnson's imposing size, golden halo, and dominant position over the depictions, at his feet, of the cramped hold of a slave ship are all visual devices that suggest moral victory over oppression and inequality—particularly poignant since Johnson was born in Texas to parents who were former slaves. By selecting a boxer as his subject, Donkor acknowledges the ways in which nineteenth- and twentieth-century European and American perceptions stereo-

fig. 76 | OPPOSITE

[plate 59]
Fodé Camara
born 1958, Senegal
Acculturation II (detail)
2000
Acrylic on canvas
190.5 x 127.2 cm
(75 x 50 1/16 in.)
National Museum of African
Art, Smithsonian Institution,
museum purchase, 2001-4-1

typed African and diasporan peoples in terms of their physical prowess and their roles as entertainers. The composition also draws inspiration from a well-known nineteenth-century lithograph by Théodore Géricault, depicting a legendary fight between a black and a white boxer.[4]

In a related approach, Cortor's work includes the image of Johnson amid a collection of clothing, personal items, and memorabilia that reflect a history of heroic struggles by African American boxers from the 1920s to the 1940s. A robe with the lettering TIGER FLOWERS refers to Theodore Flowers, the first African American middleweight champion in the 1920s. The headline DEMPSEY VS WILLS SIGNED, emblazoned across the black newspaper *The Chicago Defender,* recalls the public and controversial negotiations between the white heavyweight champion Jack Dempsey and the "colored" champion Harry Wills to agree to a match. Although they signed the agreement touted in the newspaper headline, the fight never took place. Pinned to the wall is a newspaper clipping of the heavyweight champion Joe Louis in his Army uniform during World War II. Cortor's *Still Life* pays homage to black sportsmen who were seen as heroes in the black community. Their bouts, fought outside and inside the ring, were often politically as well as racially charged, mirroring the struggles for equality at work in the larger community.

The Senegalese artist Fodé Camara employs a different kind of gesture—one that conceals rather than combats—to investigate long-standing concerns about identity and belonging in the postcolonial world. In *Acculturation II* (FIG. 76, PLATE 59), a boldly colored, powerfully rendered male figure holds up a blank document to conceal his face. The gesture is deliberate, the posture solid, possibly suggesting a form of passive resistance or signaling the tensions surrounding an uncertain, unknown future. Is the figure emotionally removed from the scene or poised to lower the blank slate and engage with us? The artist, as is so often the case, leaves such deliberations to the viewer.

Both appropriation and concealment are devices used by the South African artist Senzeni Marasela in her series of delicately embroidered works on cotton entitled *Covering Sarah* (FIG. 77, PLATE 60). The artist embroiders on pieces of cloth that recall napkins, table runners, and other domestic items. The act of sewing reflects feminist histories and experiences through the idiom of women's work. In this compelling triptych, Marasela explores her own history as a black woman of some privilege in South Africa; her father was a police officer and she attended private schools, though that did not prevent her being discriminated against by virtue of her race.[5] Marasela, speaking about her art, has discussed how she works through her history of feeling both love for her mother, who is schizophrenic, and her mother's loss.[6]

Amid the ambivalence that Marasela expresses with regard to her personal journey, she examines ideas of Western exploitation and racial stereotyping through imagery associated with Saartjie (Sarah) Baartman, a black South African woman who was exhibited in early nineteenth-century British and European sideshows as the "Hottentot Venus." Baartman's popularity as a sideshow attraction was due, in part, to her "exotic" origins and her distinctive physique, including her prominent buttocks, which contrasted markedly with Western notions of the feminine ideal. Baartman's bodily features were thought by some Westerners to be physical proof that black women were hypersexual and therefore deviant. After her untimely death in 1815, Parisian scientists dissected her corpse, removed her genitals, and preserved her remains and a plaster cast of her body in the Musée de l'Homme in Paris as what they asserted was "scientific proof" of Western perceptions of the "savage nature" of Africans. Baartman's remains were finally repatriated to South Africa in 2002, renewing interest in her story. In the simple gesture of covering Baartman's body, Marasela removes Sarah from this history of voyeuristic Western exploitation and clothes her, albeit in attire (a full skirt, an apron,

fig. 77

[plate 60]
Senzeni Marasela
born 1977, South Africa
Covering Sarah (detail)
2009–10
Cloth, thread
Triptych, each: 45.7 x
45.7 cm (18 x 18 in.)
National Museum of African
Art, Smithsonian Institution,
museum purchase, 2012-3-1

fig. 78

[plate 69]
Robert Colescott
1925–2009, United States
Death of a Mulatto Woman
(detail)
1991
Acrylic on canvas
213.3 x 182.8 cm (84 x 72 in.)
The Collection of Camille O.
and William H. Cosby Jr.

and a head scarf) often associated with South African domestic workers—a profession with its own history of social and economic exploitation. In this way the artist communicates both her own feeling of loss due to her mother's illness and the loss that black children experience throughout South Africa, as they are forced to grow up without their mothers who work outside the home in the service of other families.[7] Marasela joins many contemporary female artists around the globe who have engaged with and reimagined the horrific story of Sarah Baartman and, through their interventions, attempted to heal the indignities in this episode of history.[8]

Robert Colescott casts broad blame, a withering gaze, and a sense of humor on the prevalence of racial stereotypes in his deliberate exaggeration of the female form at the center of *Death of a Mulatto Woman* (FIGS. 40, 78, PLATE 69). In this jarring scene the artist ruminates on the trope of the "tragic mulatto," a legacy of the racial and sexual violence of American slavery. A stock character in nineteenth- and early twentieth-century American fiction, the tragic mulatto embodies the notion that the mixing of black and white blood results in an impossible conflict of being. Unable to fit in either society, he or she lives an ambivalent life that cannot be reconciled except in death. Colescott unites whites and blacks as both mourners and voyeuristic spectators who view the woman, and he suggests her mixed ancestry, as she is "thrust across two continents"— Africa to the right, as the face of a female figure in a purple dress, and Europe emerging in the lower left corner—as a "reminder of the mixed ancestry of many African Americans."[9] While the tragic mulatto is a contrived character, Colescott reminds us of the politics of race that continue to haunt our culture, which was built on fragile, and meaningless, racial divisions.

Erika Ranee Cosby's *Hanging Out to Dry* reflects the artist's study of stereotypical images of African Americans in American popular culture and her frustration at the scarcity of black dolls during her childhood in the late 1960s, when such stereotypes had somewhat been eradicated (FIG. 79, PLATE 71). According to the artist, the painting was her "ode to the scarcity—and to the plight—of the black doll. It may also suggest a loaded history of adversity and violence inflicted by the white populace onto generations of African Americans. The positioning of the dolls hanging from a clothesline, in an up-side-down trajectory as they are suspended in perpetuity, suggests an uncertain future status. The expressionistic paint rendering and predominant use of red are a visceral in-terpretation of the persistent and relentless distortion of black imagery in our culture."[10]

Human drama and community concern are explored in a number of artworks de-picting people as they gather together to observe, to commiserate, to spread the word, and to speculate about the impact of events that mark their lives. The causes and reper-cussions of the death of a respected cleric are explored by Palmer Hayden in *When Tricky Sam Shot Father Lamb* (PLATE 67). Bruce Onobrakpeya's *Have You Heard?* consid-ers the stunned reaction of Nigerians to the end of their country's civil war, which had arisen in 1967 from ethnic and religious rivalries over the new oil industry (PLATE 61). Although the war ended in 1970, Nigerians were left to wonder if peace could really be secured in the wake of some one hundred thousand military casualties and between five hundred thousand and two million civilian deaths.

Many South African artists have commented in their work on the turmoil and vio-lence that were promoted during the period of apartheid and that remain a concern in the face of current social and economic inequalities in the country. David Koloane's *Moon and Dog,* for example, presents a harrowing view of the vast divide between urban and township life during apartheid through the depiction of a stray dog howling on the edge of the city (PLATE 62). The artist considered such dogs "agents of violence" that threatened township residents who were forced to travel from township to city for

fig. 79

[plate 71]
Erika Ranee Cosby
born 1965, United States
Hanging Out to Dry (detail)
1991
Shellac, oil, charcoal, pencil
on canvas
183.3 x 212.8 cm
(72 1/8 x 83 3/4 in.)
The Collection of Camille O.
and William H. Cosby Jr.

fig. 80

[plate 64]
William Kentridge
born 1955, South Africa
Head (detail)
1994
Charcoal, pastel, and
tempera on paper
50 x 66.3 cm
(19 11/16 x 26 1/8 in.)
National Museum of African
Art, Smithsonian Institution,
purchased with funds pro-
vided by the Annie Laurie
Aitken Endowment, 98-12-1

work.[11] The artist Willie Bester, who was once imprisoned under apartheid for loitering, memorializes the history of harassment and oppression in South Africa's black settlements in *The Notorious Green Car,* with its mesh window screen that recalls the screens in police vehicles (PLATE 63). William Kentridge relates these specific histories to larger, shared human dramas in a work that focuses on a head, pictured as part of a corpse, that is outlined in reddish chalk—a crime scene one could find anywhere in the world. The viewpoint recalls the round sight of a sniper's rifle (FIG. 80, PLATE 64), but a rock in the foreground suggests the deadly potential of a different weapon.

Violence and conflict are mutual concerns that are aestheticized in different ways by the South African artist Johannes Phokela and the African American artist Keith Morrison. From a distance, Phokela's *Cuts* looks like an abstract arrangement of concentric red lines (FIG. 81, PLATE 65). Upon closer examination, however, one sees that the artist has slashed the canvas and stitched up the gashes, which drip red paint as if from fresh wounds. It is a viscerally powerful work, yet a repeat pattern of gold frames overlays these wounds—a visual device that perhaps allowed the artist to remove himself from the violence he saw inflicted on his fellow citizens. Morrison's *Zanzibar* is also a study in contrasts (FIG. 82, PLATE 68), though its emotional impact is indirect. In this abstract composition, a dominant dark blue background is interrupted by the diagonal movement of a wide band of red, which, Driskell writes, "symbolizes the political conflict the artist encountered in East Africa."[12]

The dynamics of power—social, political, economic, racial—unite the artworks in this section. In these works the artists explore the human capacity to dominate or subjugate others; to contest, appropriate, or undermine authority; to identify injustices; to subvert the status quo; and to hold an abiding hope in the possibility for positive change that comes through an embrace of social justice and true equality. By tapping into our minds and our hearts, this art holds the power to transform.

NOTES

1. See, for example, Weber (1964) on power and authority; Simmel (1950) on domination, legitimation, and consent; and Comaroff and Comaroff (1991) on hegemony and ideology. Arens and Karp (1989, xiv) argue that expressions of power should be explored as dynamic "cultural resources that produce structure and action."

2. Ater 2011, 33.

3. Ibid., 32.

4. For an image of Géricault's lithograph, see "*Boxers,* 1818," Metropolitan Museum of Art, New York, http://www.metmuseum.org/toah/works-of-art/22.63.28.

5. B. Thompson 2008, 294.

6. Senzeni Marasela, quoted in B. Thompson 2008, 293.

7. Ibid., 293–96.

8. For more on the historical and artistic responses to the "Hottentot Venus," see Willis 2010.

9. Driskell 2001, 142.

10. Erika Ranee Cosby, e-mail message to Adrienne L. Childs, December 27, 2013.

11. David Koloane, quoted in Williamson and Jamal 1996, 56.

12. Driskell 2001, 161.

fig. 81 | OPPOSITE

[plate 65]
Johannes Phokela
born 1966, South Africa
Cuts (detail)
1990
Acrylic and string on canvas
211 x 211 cm
(83 1/16 x 83 1/16 in.)
National Museum of African
Art, Smithsonian Institution,
purchased with funds
provided by the Smithsonian
Collections Acquisition
Program, 96-24-1

fig. 82 | RIGHT

[plate 68]
Keith Morrison
born 1942, Jamaica
Zanzibar
1981
Watercolor
58.5 x 77.3 cm
(23 x 30 3/8 in.)
The Collection of Camille O.
and William H. Cosby Jr.

plate 57

Ousmane Sow
born 1935, Senegal
*Toussaint Louverture et la
vieille esclave (Toussaint
Louverture and the Elderly
Slave)*
1989
Mixed media (iron, earth,
jute, straw)
220 x 100 x 110 cm
(86 5/8 x 39 3/8 x 43 5/16 in.)
National Museum of African
Art, Smithsonian Institution,
museum purchase, through
exchange from Emil Eisenberg,
and Mr. and Mrs. Norman
Robbins, and with funds from
Stuart Bohart and Barbara
Portman, 2009-8-1

plate 58

Godfried Donkor
born 1964, Ghana
From Slave to Champ I
1992
Mixed media on paper
62.7 x 47.5 cm
(24 11/16 x 18 11/16 in.)
National Museum of African
Art, Smithsonian Institution,
purchased with funds
provided by the Smithsonian
Collections Acquisition
Program, 96-21-2

Fodé Camara
born 1958, Senegal
Acculturation II
2000
Acrylic on canvas
190.5 x 127.2 cm
(75 x 50 1/16 in.)
National Museum of African
Art, Smithsonian Institution,
museum purchase, 2001-4-1

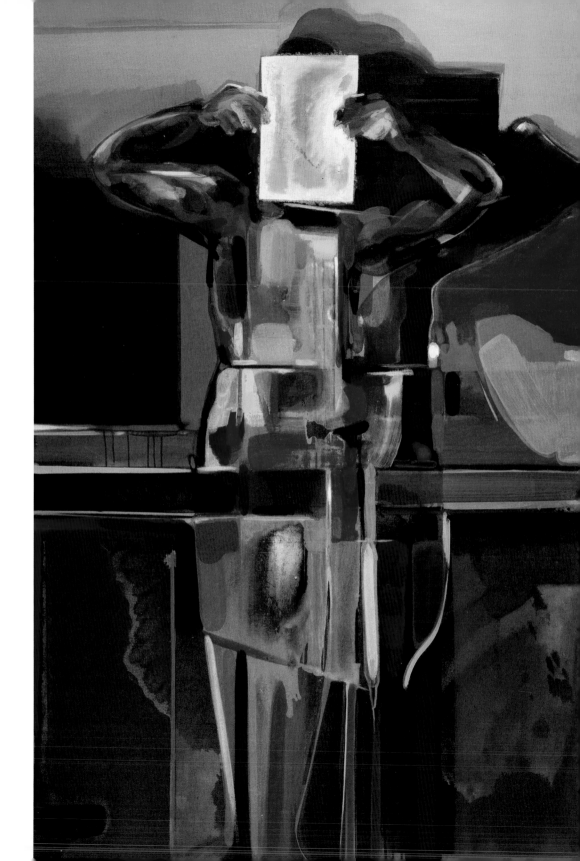

plate 60 | OPPOSITE

Senzeni Marasela
born 1977, South Africa
Covering Sarah
2009–10
Cloth, thread
Triptych, each:
45.7 x 45.7 cm (18 x 18 in.)
National Museum of African
Art, Smithsonian Institution,
museum purchase, 2012-3-1

plate 61 | RIGHT

Bruce Onobrakpeya
born 1932, Nigeria
Have You Heard?
1970
Deep etching on paper
69.5 x 50.9 cm
(27 3/8 x 20 1/16 in.)
National Museum of African
Art, Smithsonian Institution,
gift of the George I. and Jean
Lythcott family, 93-19-1

plate 62

David Koloane
born 1938, South Africa
Moon and Dog
1995
Acrylic on canvas
109.3 x 104 cm
(43 1/16 x 40 15/16 in.)
National Museum of African
Art, Smithsonian Institution,
museum purchase, 96-31-1

plate 63

Willie Bester
born 1956, South Africa
The Notorious Green Car
1995
Metal, paint, burlap, glass,
Plexiglas, bone, plastic, cloth,
wood, rubber, paper, wire
175 x 100 x 21 cm
(68 7/8 x 39 3/8 x 8 1/4 in.)
National Museum of African
Art, Smithsonian Institution,
museum purchase, 96-26-1

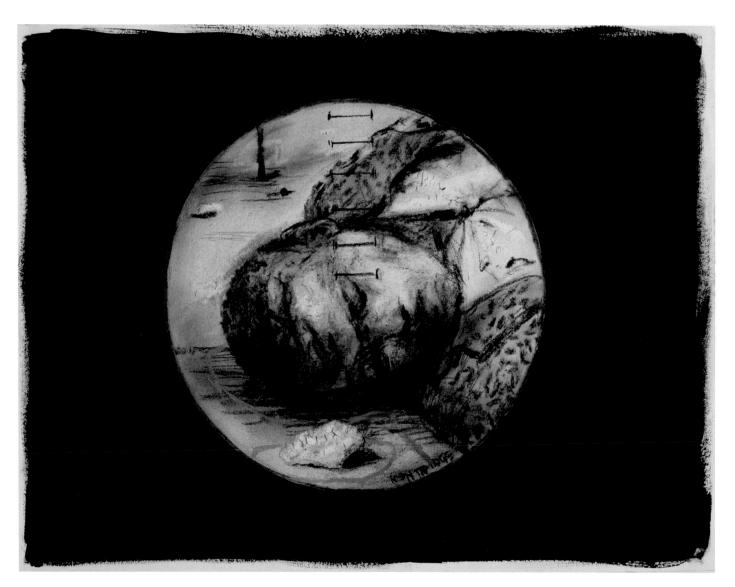

plate 64 | LEFT

William Kentridge
born 1955, South Africa
Head
1994
Charcoal, pastel, and
tempera on paper
50 x 66.3 cm
(19 11/16 x 26 1/8 in.)
National Museum of African
Art, Smithsonian Institution,
purchased with funds pro-
vided by the Annie Laurie
Aitken Endowment, 98-12-1

plate 65 | OPPOSITE

Johannes Phokela
born 1966, South Africa
Cuts
1990
Acrylic and string on canvas
211 x 211 cm
(83 1/16 x 83 1/16 in.)
National Museum of African
Art, Smithsonian Institution,
purchased with funds pro-
vided by the Smithsonian
Collections Acquisition
Program, 96-24-1

plate 68

Keith Morrison
born 1942, Jamaica
Zanzibar
1981
Watercolor
58.5 x 77.3 cm (23 x 30 3/8 in.)
The Collection of Camille O.
and William H. Cosby Jr.

Robert Colescott
1925–2009, United States
Death of a Mulatto Woman
1991
Acrylic on canvas
213.3 x 182.8 cm
(84 x 72 in.)
The Collection of Camille O.
and William H. Cosby Jr.

Memory, Family, and the Domestic Sphere

THE DOMESTIC SPHERE comprises spaces where we live and nurture, and where we often become our most authentic selves. It defines a social place that engages the inner world of family and the outer, public world. Repositories for both utilitarian and aesthetic objects, domestic spaces are imbued with our own sense of personal and cultural identity. Artists have long represented domestic interiors, imagining them as spaces for reflection, family celebrations, aesthetic expression, memory, and more. African and African American artists and craftspeople have used domestic objects and environments to define powerful aspects of identity formation and to shape cultural practice.

155

In addition to figurative works of art, African artists have created exceptionally beautiful, well-crafted, and significant personal objects designed to fulfill utilitarian, cultural, and aesthetic requirements. As items that were made to be seen as well as used, objects such as stools, chairs, neck rests, pipes, utensils, and containers functioned within the contexts of ordinary daily life—but they communicated much more. A highly decorated cup, mirror case, ladle, or bowl (PLATE 72, PLATE 73, PLATE 74, PLATE 76), for example, likely fulfilled functional requirements, but aesthetic elaboration may well have removed such objects from daily use, reserving them, instead, for special occasions and distinguishing them as visual markers of the refined taste, high position, or economic status of those who commissioned and owned such objects.

African artists bring their own creativity to bear, employing innovation and adopting new forms and materials that alter or challenge established conventions and set new formal, aesthetic, and functional standards for so-called traditional objects. One can easily admire the inventiveness of a Teke potter who makes a clear connection between the body of a ceramic vessel and the female form, suggested by the pot's curvaceous volumes and prominent handles, which seem to rest on swelling hips supported by firmly planted feet (FIG. 85, PLATE 75). Even the language used to describe pottery vessels—they have a "neck," a "body," and "feet"—confirms what those who have worked with African potters know: that in form and process pots relate to ideas about agency and the human body and (at least in the case of pots serving traditional functions) to notions about the creation of life and the capacities of power and transformation. The latter notions are often linked to the activity and the identities of potters—who, in Africa, are predominantly female.

The creative, nurturing role of women in traditional African contexts is also reflected in objects that image the female form. A lidded bowl with figures, made in the

fig. 83 | OVERLEAF, LEFT

[plate 94]
William Pajaud
born 1925, United States
Mujer con Maiz, Tortilla Maker 4
From the Mujeres series
1973
Oil on canvas
149.5 x 122 cm
(58 7/8 x 48 in.)
The Collection of Camille O. and William H. Cosby Jr.

fig. 84 | OVERLEAF, RIGHT

[plate 82]
Moustapha Dimé
1952–1998, Senegal
Femme Sérère (Serer Woman)
1992
Wood, metal
145 x 49 cm
(57 1/16 x 19 5/16 in.)
National Museum of African Art, Smithsonian Institution, gift of Marcia and Irwin Hersey, 2004-15-1

fig. 85

[plate 75]
Teke artist, Democratic
Republic of the Congo,
Republic of the Congo
Vessel
Early 20th century
Ceramic, pigment
25.7 x 21 x 9 cm
(10 1/8 x 8 1/4 x 3 9/16 in.)
National Museum of African
Art, Smithsonian Institution,
museum purchase, 85-4-1

early twentieth century by the Yoruba master artist Olowe of Ise, signals the central role of women in social and ritual contexts (PLATE 77). This prestige bowl, owned by someone of high status, likely held kola nuts, which are presented to guests in a traditional gesture of hospitality and offered to deities during rituals. Such objects underscore the importance of leisure time and socializing, when family and friends gather together. The prominent head, which reflects Yoruba concepts of the head as a locus of destiny and of ritual import, allows the artist an expansive surface for carving culturally significant embellishments—an elaborate coiffure and scarification marks on the face and body—that, in addition to prominent breasts and a well-balanced form, link physical beauty to ideal moral qualities.

In certain parts of West Africa, gourd containers serve as surrogates for the female body, and pyro-engraved motifs decorate the vessels much as female bodies were traditionally ornamented (PLATE 78). In these and other cases, such as among the Moba of northern Togo, the surface embellishments of containers, utensils, furnishings, and spaces linked to women reflect a shared, gender-based aesthetic system that reinforces female identity and the creative capacities of women and women's work.[1]

Such ideas likely influenced the contemporary Senegalese artist Moustapha Dimé in the creation of his sculpture *Femme Sérère* (FIG. 84, PLATE 82). He fashioned his Serer woman out of ordinary utensils—mortars, a pestle, wooden bowls—that a Senegalese woman might use in daily food preparation. In so doing, the artist created a powerful, poetic statement about valuing the significant contributions women make to family and community.

Specific cultural practices can imbue certain personal objects with significance—connected to ceremonies, rituals, status, gender, and identity—that extends well beyond the utilitarian. A stool made by a Luguru artist is distinguished by its high backrest in the form of a stylized female torso with small, projecting breasts (FIG. 86, PLATE 79). The head is embellished with a crested hairstyle and there are small scarification marks on either side of the face. Scholars have suggested that such stools are possibly related to female ancestors of chiefs and other notables, and reflect the prominence of matrilineal societies in parts of Tanzania. More recent research on Tanzanian arts also documents the stools' connections to initiation rites and their function as seats of power akin to altars on which smaller ritual objects are placed.[2]

Personal objects evolve over time, and they reflect life histories of ownership and use. In traditional contexts of use, an Asante stool symbolizes the soul of its owner and may be tipped over when not in use (FIG. 87, PLATE 80). It can also serve as the focus of a family shrine at the person's death, when the stool may be blackened and receive libations as offerings. Over the years stools made by Asante and other Akan artists have also become popular in the tourist trade, where they are much admired for their elegant form. All Asante stools recall the legendary Golden Stool, the first Asante chief's gilded stool, believed to have descended from the sky, which is never sat upon but which contains the spirit of the Asante kingdom.

In many of the works in the Cosby collection, the public presentation of the private sphere offers a complex depiction of African American life as it is played out in the details of the everyday (FIG. 83, PLATE 94). From the mundane to the magical, inanimate objects often carry the power to signify the personal and cultural well beyond the limits of their original functions. For the artist David C. Driskell, the chair is a motif that has informed his art since the 1960s, when he started collecting American furniture. *The Green Chair* (FIG. 88, PLATE 95) is part of Driskell's Americana series. On one level, Driskell's painting represents the form and function of an ordinary object that provides support, stability, and comfort. However, the expressive handling of the green paint and the vivid

fig. 86 | LEFT

[plate 79]
Luguru artist, Tanzania
High-backed stool
Early 20th century
Wood
80 x 38.1 x 37.5 cm
(31 1/2 x 15 x 14 3/4 in.)
National Museum of African
Art, Smithsonian Institution,
gift of Robert and Nancy
Nooter, 89-10-1

fig. 87 | OPPOSITE, BOTTOM

[plate 80]
Asante artist, Ghana
Stool
Mid- to late 19th century
Wood
23.7 x 39.4 x 20.3 cm
(9 5/16 x 15 1/2 x 8 in.)
National Museum of African
Art, Smithsonian Institution,
acquisition grant from the
James Smithson Society,
89-8-3

fig. 88 | RIGHT

[plate 95]
David C. Driskell
born 1931, United States
The Green Chair
From the Americana series
1978
Acrylic on canvas
101.5 x 61 cm (40 x 24 in.)
The Collection of Camille O.
and William H. Cosby Jr.

decorative embellishment of the interior space emphasize the ornamental over the functional. The chairs in Driskell's series possess their own spirit, or what he has called "their own lively domain."[3] By the time Driskell painted *The Green Chair* in 1978, he had begun to add West African chairs and stools to his collection of American furniture. His African and African American collections were never conceptualized as separate; rather, they worked together as an ensemble that embodied his African-centered and cosmopolitan worldview. Consequently, *The Green Chair* reflects the domestic and the decorative as well as notions of social elevation, power, and kingship inherent in selected traditional African stools and thrones. For Driskell, echoes of African ancestral underpinnings are present in all aspects of his life and artistry.

Other African American artists represented in the Cosby collection have explored the inner life of inanimate domestic objects through the language of still-life painting. A European tradition dating back centuries, the still-life genre has continued to resonate to the present day. The representation of an artful gathering of objects, often flowers or fruit, can evoke history, memory, traditions, and the sensibilities of everyday life. Loïs Mailou Jones explored the charm of the French provincial interior in *Nature Morte aux Geraniums* (FIG. 89, PLATE 96). The painting includes lush and colorful renderings of local fruits and flowers as well as fabrics and ceramics typical of the French countryside, where Jones painted during annual summer visits. Jones, whose work shows the influence of Paul Cézanne and Vincent van Gogh, was a pioneer in expanding the international presence of African American artists.

That same desire to create an aesthetically pleasing home environment is explored in the poignant depictions of post-apartheid township life by the contemporary South African artist Zwelethu Mthethwa. A large-format color photograph, for example, presents a portrait of a woman, dressed in church attire, standing inside her modest dwelling (FIG. 6, PLATE 81). She has decorated her home with posters, magazine covers, and photographs, and has stacked housewares and recycled consumer products into patterns. In doing so, she has revealed a lively sense of interior design and asserted her human dignity despite her humble circumstances.[4]

In Romare Bearden's masterful collages of African American domestic life, women embody the mysteries of nature and nurture, serving as mothers, muses, servants, mystics, and conjurers. From rural scenes to urban subjects, much of Bearden's work chronicles the intimate lives of African Americans as they moved along the axis from south to north in the Great Migration. The improvisational structure and evocative juxtapositions of his formal technique draw on the poetry of African American vernacular culture. Although Bearden's images speak to larger culture ways, they are rooted in his own experiences and memories. Remnants of his childhood in Mecklenburg County, North Carolina, frequently surface in his female figures. In *Magic Garden* (PLATE 98), the god-

fig. 89 | OPPOSITE, TOP

[plate 96]
Loïs Mailou Jones
1905–1998, United States
Nature Morte aux Geraniums
(detail)
1952
Oil on canvas
73.3 x 59.8 cm
(28 7/8 x 23 1/2 in.)
The Collection of Camille O.
and William H. Cosby Jr.

fig. 90 | OPPOSITE, BOTTOM

[plate 99]
Romare Bearden
1911–1988, United States
Harlem Brownstone (detail)
1980
Collage on Masonite
75.8 x 101.5 cm
(29 7/8 x 40 in.)
The Collection of Camille O.
and William H. Cosby Jr.

desslike woman holding a basket of flowers in one hand and offering a stem with small blooms in the other stands within the confines of a lush garden. Although she is outdoors, she presides within the walls of this private space. Drawn from Bearden's childhood recollections of Maudel Sleet, a woman whose abundant garden provided the artist with a lifetime of fertile memories and inspirations, the figure recalls both traditions of black southern life and the mysterious and spiritual connections Bearden saw between women and the natural world.[5]

In *Harlem Brownstone* (FIGS. 5, 90, PLATE 99), Bearden has moved north to an urban interior, signified by the New York City skyline pictured on the wall. In the well-appointed room we find a group of African American women around a family table. One combs another's hair in a traditional domestic ritual that often animates black home life, while still another sits stoically at the table. The face of the seated woman is made up of a collaged Baule (Côte d'Ivoire) mask. From Bearden's first forays into collage in the early 1960s, he used the image of an African mask, either whole or fragmented, to form faces in his compositions. This woman of indeterminate age suggests another female type that recurs in Bearden's ongoing exploration of black folklore—the conjure woman. A character born in black diasporan mythology, the conjure woman was a multifaceted figure of spirituality and power; healer, soothsayer, herbalist, and witch, she appears in various incarnations in Bearden's work, bringing with her memories and the magic of black folk culture. *Harlem Brownstone* presents the kind of interplay of tradition, mysticism, and the everyday that often characterizes Bearden's southern scenes. The distance between the North and the South collapses as Bearden's chronicle of African American life depicts the transcendent nature of black folkways. Bearden's domestic scenes do not present an inherently racial domain; rather, through the quiet moments of the African American experience, he reveals the enchantment of everyday life.

In both African and African American communities, life unfolds amid the objects, actions, and spaces of daily life and the knowledge and memories associated with them. Indeed, the creation of Africa's arts reflects long-standing histories of knowledge, technical expertise, and aesthetic concepts that are passed down in various ways to succeeding generations. In many African societies, artistic traditions were the responsibility of specific lineages, and the transmission of this knowledge was a process of hands-on learning and apprenticeship. Objects thus serve as repositories of knowledge about changing forms, techniques, materials, motifs, and contexts of creation and use.

While steeped in a long history, African textiles today—in both urban and rural settings—are contemporary, global, and dynamic. The knowledge associated with African textile traditions reflects the continent's history of trade and the circulation of people, ideas, materials, and contexts that over time inspired both continuity and innovation in the textile arts. As powerful communicators of status, gender, and accomplishment in Africa, many textiles are connected to public presentations of self (PLATE 83). Thus they are rich in content, and they create identity and meaning through their forms, materials, and modes of display. The messages conveyed through these ever-changing African art forms are similar to those articulated elsewhere in the world, emphasizing shared ways that dress and the body are used for creative expression.

Africa's textile artists are masters of technique and design. Broadloom, narrow-strip, and factory-printed textiles evince the hand of talented artisans who imbue their cloths with bold colors, complex motifs, and wonderful patterning—linear, geometric, naturalistic, and abstract—employing weft-float, embroidered, appliqué, resist, and print techniques (FIG. 91, PLATE 84). Among textiles' many contexts of use, they serve as men's and women's wrappers; as commemorative cloths for funerary rites or to honor notable public figures (PLATE 87; PLATE 89; PLATE 90; FIG. 92, PLATE 91); and as emblems of

fig. 91 | OPPOSITE, TOP

[plate 84]
Kuba artist, Shoowa group,
Democratic Republic of
the Congo
Design cloth (detail)
Mid-20th century
Raffia, dye
48.3 x 30.5 cm (19 x 12 in.)
National Museum of African
Art, Smithsonian Institution,
bequest of Eliot Elisofon,
73-7-466

fig. 92 | OPPOSITE, BOTTOM

[plate 91]
Sotiba Factory
Dakar, Senegal
Factory-printed cloth
featuring image of
Malcolm X (detail)
Late 20th century
Cotton, dye
116.4 x 142 cm
(45 13/16 x 55 7/8 in.)
National Museum of African
Art, Smithsonian Institution,
gift of the Wil and Irene Petty
Collection, 2008-5-62

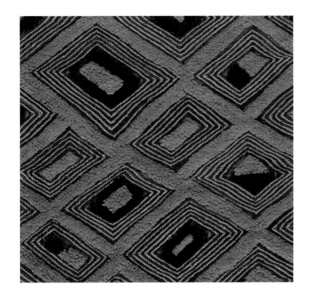

power, status, and accomplishment (PLATE 90, PLATE 92, PLATE 93). The extraordinary costumes and textiles of the African continent—from ensembles to wrappers, to wall hangings, to headwear and fabric accessories—attest to the exceptional diversity of Africa's textile arts.

African textiles are far from static, despite their manner of presentation in most museum contexts. Rather, textiles are performed, kinetic, and three-dimensional, worn on and manipulated by the body and thus moved through space in their contexts of use and display. A man's kente wrapper is composed of from seventeen to twenty-one strips of cloth woven on a narrow-strip loom (PLATE 85, PLATE 86). It is worn toga-style, over the left shoulder, in south-central Ghana. It is continually adjusted and rewrapped as the man walks, works, or dances. He may also briefly lower the shoulder portion as a sign of respect when in the presence of royalty. A woman, too, will periodically adjust her wrapper, tightening the folds securely around her waist or fashioning a wider waistband to raise the hemline when she walks through water or a muddy patch. A shoulder wrap can be pulled up to protect the head in inclement weather. These regular adjustments are part of the aesthetic experience of wearing and enjoying African textiles in motion.

The mythic nature of the everyday is at the core of the African American family quilt. The Cosbys have been particularly drawn to the quilt as a form of familial and cultural tradition, and they have amassed a large collection that ranges from family heirlooms to fine art. According to Bill Cosby, "Quilts tell a story of life."[6] One of the Cosby family's most treasured quilts was made in the early 1960s by Clara Elizabeth Jackson Carter, Camille Cosby's maternal grandmother, who lived in Shores, Virginia (PLATE 102). The Cosbys also own a quilt by the next-generation quilter Catherine Hanks, Mrs. Carter's daughter and the mother of Camille Cosby (PLATE 103). For generations the quilts were used by family members in their daily life and thus carry the traces of the family histories that they have witnessed.

Quilt making has been a fundamental part of American domestic practice passed down largely through matrilineal lines since the Europeans first colonized North America, and enslaved African American women made quilts for both their masters' families and for their own. Scholars have long acknowledged elements of African aesthetics—such as the use of bright colors, asymmetrical patterning, and appliqué designs—in African American quilts. Quilt making, often a collective effort, fostered cultural solidarity and group identity within African American slave societies, forming bonds that were transmitted through the generations. The teaching of quilt making and the "spirit" of the quilts themselves are intimately linked to the lives of those who made and cherished these textiles.

After the Cosbys hired David C. Driskell to curate and expand their collection of African American art, he introduced them to Joseph White, a quilter in Charleston, South Carolina, whom he had met in 1975

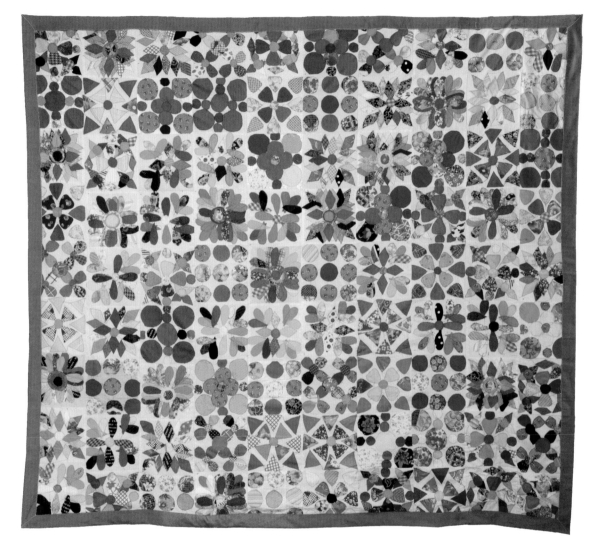

fig. 93 | OPPOSITE

[plate 104]
Joseph White
1907–n.d., United States
Quilt
c. 1970
Collected scrap fabric
266.8 x 238.8 cm
(105 x 94 in.)
The Collection of Camille O.
and William H. Cosby Jr.

while doing research for the exhibition and publication *Two Centuries of Black American Art.* White, an African American man who had learned to quilt from his mother, began quilting late in life. White's brightly colored quilts with traditional American patterns were well known in his community (FIG. 93, PLATE 104). In the 1980s the Cosbys purchased more than twenty-five quilts from White, demonstrating the value they placed on supporting the African American practitioners of this culturally significant tradition. Another male quilt artist, Michael Cummings, is represented in the Cosby collection. *African Jazz #4* (PLATE 105), from the artist's African Jazz series, is a mixed-media pictorial quilt, depicting musicians whose features are inspired in part by African masks. The narrative quilts in this series visually fuse the African roots of jazz with a dynamic, cubist-inspired space animated with African patterns and motifs.

For the Cosbys, quilts are powerful and poignant objects that honor kinship and preserve family history. In 1988, Camille Cosby commissioned *Camille's Husband's Birthday Quilt* (FIG. 18, PLATE 106) from Faith Ringgold as a special gift for Bill Cosby's birthday. Ringgold, whose story quilts join narrative with the fine and domestic arts in innovative ways, produced a patchwork quilt that combines painted images of Cosby family members at various ages and stages of life with pieced patterns of colorful fabric. The Crossroads Quilters, a mostly African American quilt-making community in Port Gibson, Mississippi, whom Camille Cosby admires and patronizes, offered to make the Cosbys a quilt in memory of their son, Ennis Cosby. Created with pieces of Ennis's clothing, the quilt features visual references to Ennis's interests, studies, and travels (FIG. 94, PLATE 107). Quilts have long been keepers of memory in the African American community, honoring the lives of ancestors while providing spiritual and physical comfort. The Cosbys were deeply touched by the gracious gesture of this community of quilters and the thoughtful commemoration of Ennis through this visually rich and meaningful art form.

The importance of remembering and honoring family in visual form is a strand that runs throughout the Cosby collection. In 2000 the artist Whitfield Lovell produced a stunning group portrait dedicated to the memory of relatives and important mentors of Bill Cosby's. Lovell's *The Promise of Learnings* (FIG. 95, PLATE 101) features Ennis Cosby standing on the left, next to Mr. Conchlin, Bill Cosby's scoutmaster; seated, from left to right, are his aunt Lillian Hite Herring, his mother Anna Pearl Hite Cosby, and his teacher Mrs. Forchek. Lovell adhered vintage books on the wood at random intervals, creating a mixed-media group portrait that is reminiscent of a patchwork quilt and suggests the emotional and intellectual contributions of these individuals to the life of Bill Cosby. This kind of assemblage, which combines found objects with ethereal, realistic portraits of often anonymous African Americans drafted on weathered wood, is Lovell's signature. Whether the portraits are drawn from Lovell's collection of unidentified historical photographs or are known family members, his haunting works speak to the ever-present spirit of the ancestors in African American life.

NOTES

1. For a discussion of this among the Moba, see also Kreamer 2007, 160–61.

2. Van Wyk 2013, 70–71.

3. David C. Driskell, quoted in McGee 2011, 39.

4. The scene in Zwelethu Mthethwa's photograph echoes Bill Cosby's description (see "Collecting Priorities: A Conversation with Bill and Camille Cosby," this volume) of his childhood home in the Richard Allen project in Philadelphia. We are grateful to our editor, Jane Bobko, for drawing this connection to our attention.

5. For Maudel Sleet and the conjure woman, see Powell et al. 2006.

6. See "Collecting Priorities," this volume.

fig. 94 | RIGHT

[plate 107]
Crossroads Quilters
Port Gibson, Mississippi
The Ennis Quilt (detail)
1997
Collected scrap fabric and
Ennis Cosby's clothing
370.8 x 294.8 cm
(146 x 116 in.)
The Collection of Camille O.
and William H. Cosby Jr.

fig. 95 | FAR RIGHT

[plate 101]
Whitfield Lovell
born 1959, United States
The Promise of Learnings
(detail)
2000
Conté crayon on board,
books
274.3 x 210.3 cm
(108 x 82 3/4 in.)
The Collection of Camille O.
and William H. Cosby Jr.

plate 72 | FAR LEFT

Kuba artist, Democratic
Republic of the Congo
Cup
Early 20th century
Wood
Diam: 12 cm (4 3/4 in.)
H: 13.4 cm (5 1/4 in.)
National Museum of African
Art, Smithsonian Institution,
museum purchase, 85-1-14

plate 73 | LEFT

Igbo artist, Nigeria
Mirror case
Mid-20th century
Wood, nails
19.4 x 10.4 x 2.5 cm
(7 5/8 x 4 1/8 x 1 in.)
National Museum of African
Art, Smithsonian Institution,
gift of Roy and Sophia Sieber
in memory of Philip L.
Ravenhill, 97-28-1

plate 76 | OPPOSITE

Lozi artist, Zambia
Bowl
Late 19th to early 20th
century
Wood
11.4 x 60.3 x 31.4 cm
(4 1/2 x 23 3/4 x 12 3/8 in.)
National Museum of African
Art, Smithsonian Institution,
acquisition grant from the
James Smithson Society,
89-8-18

plate 77 | RIGHT

Olowe of Ise
c. 1875–c. 1938, Yoruba
artist, Nigeria
Bowl with figures
Early 20th century
Wood, paint
53.8 x 25 x 35 cm
(21 3/16 x 9 13/16 x 13 3/4 in.)
National Museum of African
Art, Smithsonian Institution,
gift of Walt Disney World
Co., a subsidiary of The Walt
Disney Company, 2005-6-34

plate 78

Sara-Nar artist, Chad;
Tera, Bura, Ga'anda, Bachama,
and Hona artists, Nigeria
Bowls
Late 20th century
Gourd
Dimensions vary
National Museum of African
Art, Smithsonian Institution,
gifts of Ellen Patterson
Brown and Mildred A.
Morton, CENTER: 94-2-6;
CLOCKWISE FROM FAR LEFT:
2000-29-48, 2000-29-4,
2000-29-26, 2000-29-11,
2000-29-31

56 A 57 Seydou Keïta 99

plate 83 | OPPOSITE

Seydou Keita
1923–2001, Mali
Untitled (Odalisque)
1956–57, printed 1999
Gelatin silver print
30.5 x 40.5 cm
(12 x 15 15/16 in.)
National Museum of African
Art, Smithsonian Institution,
museum purchase,
2009-12-2

plate 84 | RIGHT

Kuba artist, Shoowa group,
Democratic Republic of
the Congo
Design cloth
Mid-20th century
Raffia, dye
48.3 x 30.5 cm (19 x 12 in.)
National Museum of African
Art, Smithsonian Institution,
bequest of Eliot Elisofon,
73-7-466

plate 85

Ewe artist, Ghana
Man's wrapper
Early 20th century
Cotton
266.7 x 182.9 cm
(105 x 72 in.)
National Museum of African
Art, Smithsonian Institution,
gift of Cynthia E. Gubernick,
70-20-78

plate 86

Gilbert "Bobbo" Ahiagble
1944–2012, Ewe artist,
Ghana
Man's wrapper
Late 20th century
Cotton, dyes
243.8 x 274.3 cm
(96 x 108 in.)
National Museum of African
Art, Smithsonian Institution,
museum purchase, 98-17-1

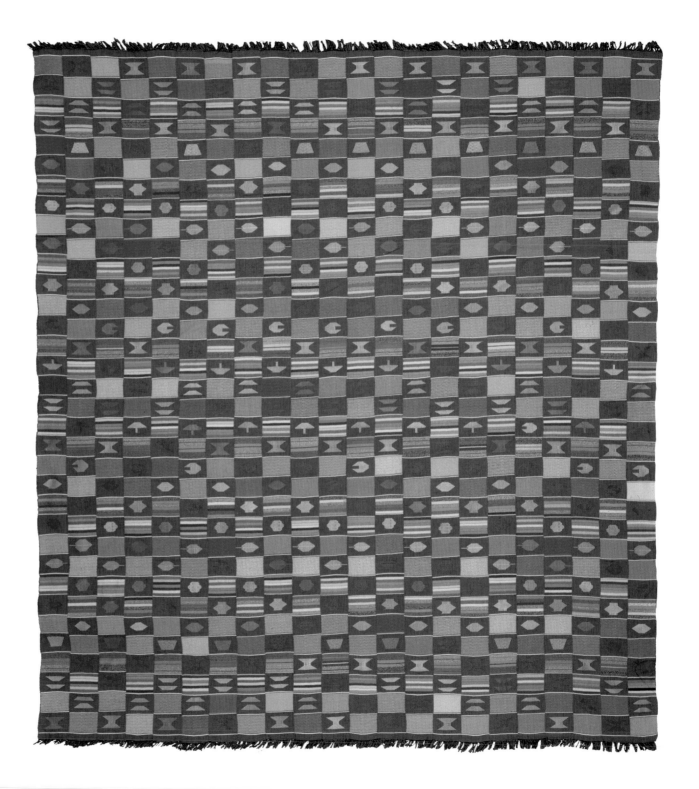

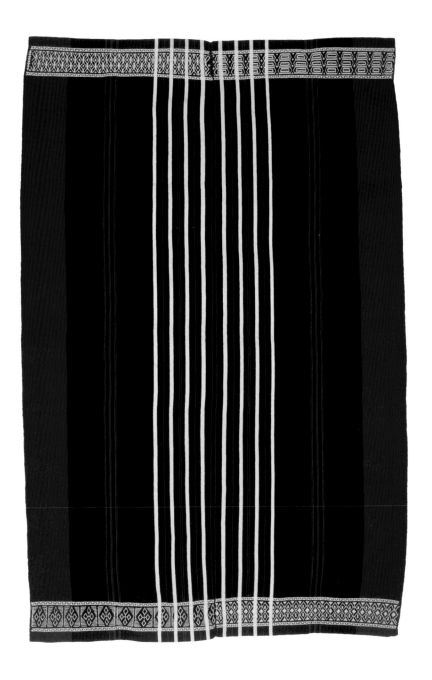

plate 87 | OPPOSITE, FAR LEFT

Felicité Rasoazanany
n.d., Merina artist,
Madagascar
Burial cloth
1996
Wild silk, mulberry silk,
cotton weft, natural dyes
220.8 x 138.5 cm
(86 15/16 x 54 1/2 in.)
National Museum of African
Art, Smithsonian Institution,
museum purchase, 2000-13-1

plate 88 | OPPOSITE, LEFT

Betsileo artist, Madagascar
Great cloth
1995
Cotton, dye
224.5 x 138.9 cm
(88 3/8 x 54 11/16 in.)
National Museum of African
Art, Smithsonian Institution,
museum purchase,
2000-13-11

plate 89 | RIGHT

Okon Akpan Abuje
born c. 1900, Anang artist,
Afaha clan, Ikot Obong
village, Akwa-Ibom State,
Nigeria
Funerary-shrine cloth
Late 1970s
Commercial cotton cloth,
cotton thread
344.8 x 153 cm
(135 3/4 x 60 1/4 in.)
National Museum of African
Art, Smithsonian Institution,
museum purchase, 84-6-9

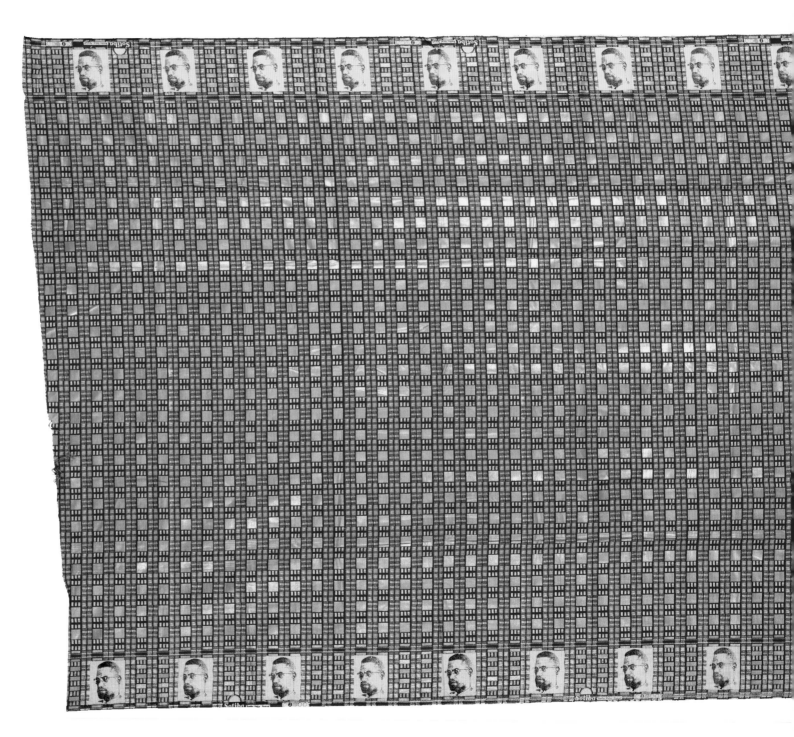

plate 90 | OPPOSITE

Designed by Prince Edu
Akenzua
born 1923, Edo peoples,
Nigeria
Commemorative cloth
for the coronation of
Aghahouwa N'Iyoba,
Akenzua's mother
1980–81
Cloth
544 x 117 cm
(214 3/16 x 46 1/16 in.)
National Museum of African
Art, Smithsonian Institution,
gift of Flora Edouwaye S.
Kaplan, 2004-10-7

plate 91 | RIGHT

Sotiba Factory
Dakar, Senegal
Factory-printed cloth featuring
image of Malcolm X
Late 20th century
Cotton, dye
116.4 x 142 cm
(45 13/16 x 55 7/8 in.)
National Museum of African
Art, Smithsonian Institution,
gift of the Wil and Irene
Petty Collection, 2008-5-62

plate 92 | OPPOSITE

Oumar Bocoum
born mid-20th century,
Fulbe artist, Mali
Marriage blanket
Late 20th century
Cotton, dye
158 x 348 cm
(62 3/16 x 137 in.)
National Museum of African
Art, Smithsonian Institution,
gift of the Ambassador
Arthur and Doctor Frances
Lewis Collection, 2011-17-8

plate 93 | RIGHT

Fante artist, Ghana
Man's wrapper
Mid- to late 20th century
Mill-woven wool,
embroidery thread
198.7 x 304.2 cm
(78 1/4 x 119 3/4 in.)
National Museum of African
Art, Smithsonian Institution,
museum purchase, 84-6-10

plate 94

William Pajaud
born 1925, United States
*Mujer con Maiz, Tortilla
Maker 4*
From the Mujeres series
1973
Oil on canvas
149.5 x 122 cm
(58 7/8 x 48 in.)
The Collection of Camille O.
and William H. Cosby Jr.

David C. Driskell
born 1931, United States
The Green Chair
From the Americana series
1978
Acrylic on canvas
101.5 x 61 cm (40 x 24 in.)
The Collection of Camille O.
and William H. Cosby Jr.

plate 96

Loïs Mailou Jones
1905–1998, United States
Nature Morte aux Geraniums
1952
Oil on canvas
73.3 x 59.8 cm
(28 7/8 x 23 1/2 in.)
The Collection of Camille O.
and William H. Cosby Jr.

plate 97

Varnette Honeywood
1950–2010, United States
Precious Memories
1984
Collage
80.8 x 55.8 cm
(31 3/4 x 22 in.)
The Collection of Camille O.
and William H. Cosby Jr.

plate 100 | OPPOSITE

Eldzier Cortor
born 1916, United States
*Homage to 466 Cherry
Street*
1987
Oil on Masonite
93.3 x 118 cm
(36 3/4 x 46 1/2 in.)
The Collection of Camille O.
and William H. Cosby Jr.

plate 101 | RIGHT

Whitfield Lovell
born 1959, United States
The Promise of Learnings
2000
Conté crayon on board,
books
274.3 x 210.3 cm
(108 x 82 3/4 in.)
The Collection of Camille O.
and William H. Cosby Jr.

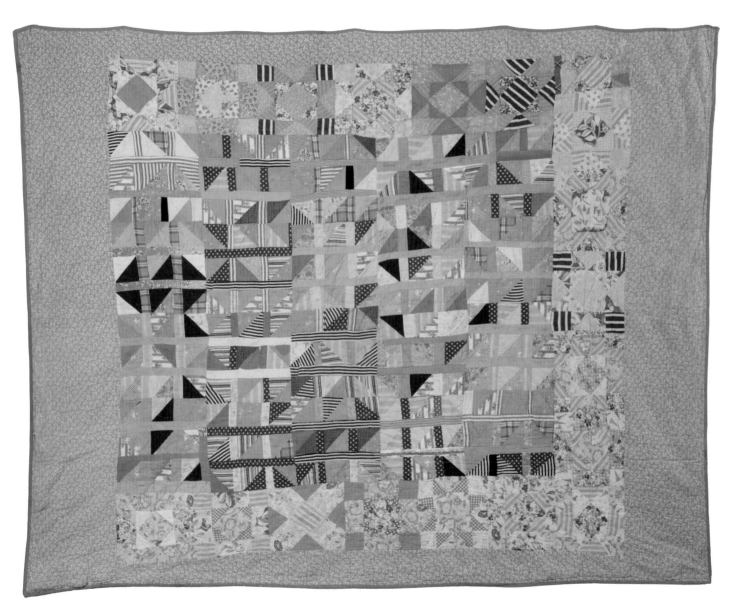

plate 102 | LEFT

Clara Elizabeth Jackson
Carter
1881–1971, United States
Quilt
1962
Mail-ordered scrap fabric
181.5 x 231.3 cm
(71 1/2 x 91 in.)
The Collection of Camille O.
and William H. Cosby Jr.

plate 103 | OPPOSITE

Catherine Hanks
born 1922, United States
Quilt
1966
Cotton fabric
122 x 210.8 cm (48 x 83 in.)
The Collection of Camille O.
and William H. Cosby Jr.

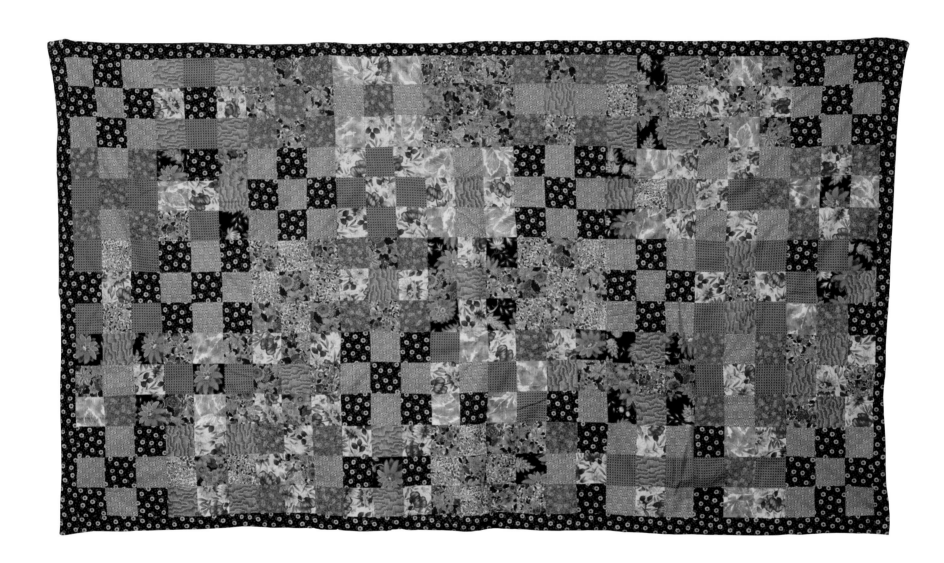

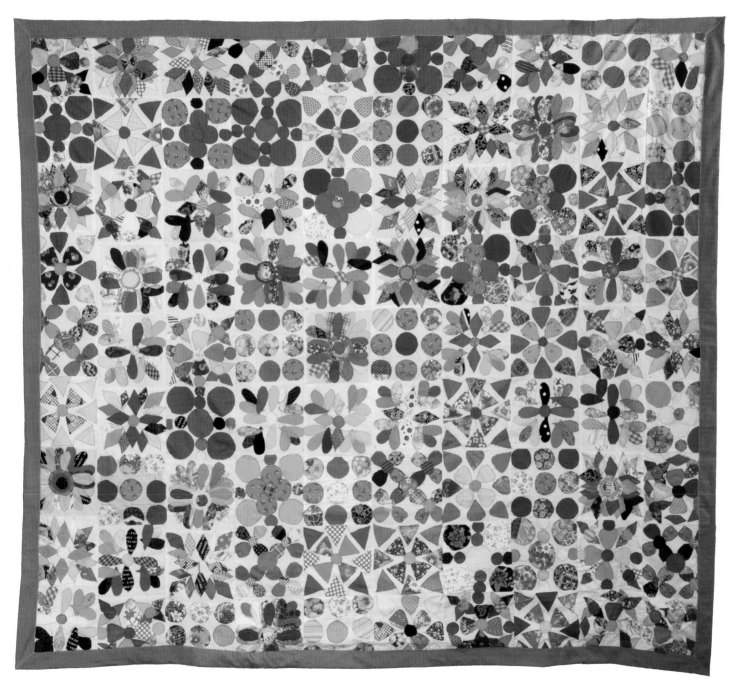

plate 104

Joseph White
1907–n.d., United States
Quilt
c. 1970
Collected scrap fabric
266.8 x 238.8 cm
(105 x 94 in.)
The Collection of Camille O.
and William H. Cosby Jr.

plate 105

Michael Cummings
born 1945, United States
African Jazz #4
From the African Jazz series
1990
Cotton synthetic with plastic
balls, metal, buttons
294.8 x 179 cm
(116 x 70 1/2 in.)
The Collection of Camille O.
and William H. Cosby Jr.

plate 106

Faith Ringgold
born 1930, United States
*Camille's Husband's
Birthday Quilt*
1988
Painted and pieced canvas
and silk
269.3 x 207.8 cm
(106 x 81 3/4 in.)
The Collection of Camille O.
and William H. Cosby Jr.

Crossroads Quilters
Port Gibson, Mississippi
The Ennis Quilt
1997
Collected scrap fabric and
Ennis Cosby's clothing
370.8 x 294.8 cm
(146 x 116 in.)
The Collection of Camille O.
and William H. Cosby Jr.

Nature as Metaphor

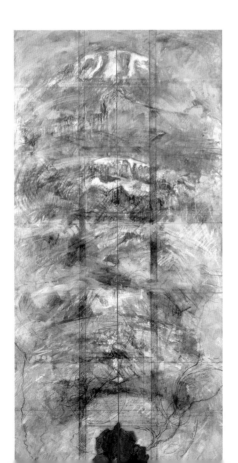

N CERTAIN WORKS OF ART in *Conversations,* nature serves as metaphor in exploring intersecting ideas about history, identity, power, knowledge, spirituality, and environmental stewardship. African and African American artistic engagement with the world ranges from naturalism to abstraction to surrealist meditations; these examine in distinctive ways the multifaceted, often flawed relationships that human beings have with one another and with the physical and intellectual environments in which they live.

Selected works of traditional African art demonstrate how artists are keen observers of the natural world and understand the complexities associated

201

with it. Among the Nuna of Burkina Faso, butterflies are harbingers of rain and thus their appearance is closely connected to the start of the farming season. Butterfly masks (PLATE 108) reflect this knowledge as well as the spiritual properties linked with nature, since this and other masks among the Nuna and related groups in the region are representations of nature spirits that combine human and animal form. Both the celestial and the terrestrial domain are suggested in the form of the butterfly mask, which merges the representation of a human head, rendered in high relief, with a huge, bird-like creature, depicted with concentric-circle eyes and a projecting, diamond-shaped bill. Three-dimensional birds and chameleons perch above the massive wings, which are ornamented with red, black, and white geometric motifs, suggesting the patterning of butterfly wings. In this region of Burkina Faso highly entertaining masquerade performances enliven ceremonial and secular occasions. They bring nature spirits into contact with domesticated village life and give humans access to the powerful and protective capacities of the natural world and its denizens.

For the Yoruba of Nigeria, traditional artworks that depict a large bird in the center of a gathering of birds symbolize the control of supernatural forces and the dominance of good over evil (PLATE 109, PLATE 110). The motif designates the power of the herbalist, who is a priest of the gods of healing, Osanyin and Erinle. Birds inhabit the dual realms of sky and earth; as birds take flight, their vantage point provides superior surveillance of the world below. These qualities are positively linked to the exceptional capacities of Yoruba kings and others, such as herbalists, whose leadership skills and specialized knowledge translate into their authority over secular and sacred domains. Through their work such individuals bring order to the world and counterbalance malevolent forces, which can also take flight—particularly at night—and threaten the world of humans.

The natural world serves contemporary African artists, too, as a rich source of

fig. 96 | OVERLEAF, LEFT

[plate 115]
Robert S. Duncanson
1821–1872, United States
Falls of Minnehaha
1862
Oil on canvas
92 x 71.8 cm
(36 1/4 x 28 1/4 in.)
The Collection of Camille O.
and William H. Cosby Jr.

fig. 97 | OVERLEAF, RIGHT

[plate 113]
Georgia Papageorge
born 1941, South Africa
*Maasai Steppe Ascending—
Convective Displacement*
1997
Oil stick and graphite on
canvas with volcanic rock
and cloth
239 x 117 cm
(94 1/8 x 46 1/16 in.)
National Museum of African
Art, Smithsonian Institution,
museum purchase, 98-19-1

fig. 98

[plate 111]
Papa Ibra Tall
born 1935, Senegal
Tapestry
1964
Cotton, wool, dye
157.5 x 226 cm (62 x 89 in.)
National Museum of African
Art, Smithsonian Institution,
gift of Robert S. McNamara,
84-7-1

metaphor. A harmonious world order, for example, is conceived through the intermingling of human and floral imagery in a brightly hued tapestry, from the 1960s, created by the Senegalese modernist Papa Ibra Tall (FIG. 98, PLATE 111). At first it is hard to discern the human forms that emerge and recede amid the highly decorative vegetation that dominates the composition. Then the eyes adjust to the ways that the central figure's head and hands, and the smaller heads to either side, are composed of the surrounding flora—a visualization of intellectual engagement in perfect balance with the natural world.

By contrast, the Ethiopian artist Alexander "Skunder" Boghossian presents a chaotic view of nature, a cosmos out of balance, in *Devil Descending* (PLATE 112). Painted in 1972, the work—along with others produced around that time—captures the instability and tensions leading up to the overthrow of the Ethiopian monarchy in 1974. A fragmented landscape composed of a jumble of geometric forms, graphic symbols, and complex imagery is set against a sky dominated by an orange-red sun, a crescent moon, and a massive predatory creature with shadowy wings outstretched. It is a surreal world clearly threatened by the evil forces set to wreak havoc upon it.

The theme of life out of balance is also explored by the South African artist Georgia Papageorge, who incorporates ground-down volcanic rock from the crater and other areas of Tanzania's Mount Kilimanjaro in *Maasai Steppe Ascending—Convective Displacement* (FIG. 97, PLATE 113). It is one of a series of works in which the artist explores the destructive effects of poor environmental stewardship, with particular emphasis on the decreasing snow cover atop the mountain owing to climate change, deforestation, and charcoal production. A ladder links sky and earth, calling to mind the difficult ascent to the summit or, possibly, the challenging path to transcendence. Papageorge's use of red cloth suggests the bloodlines that bind us to one another, to the geologic sweep of our shared history, and to our mutual obligation to ensure that our world and its natural beauties survive for the benefit of future generations. In this and other works, Papageorge meditates on the concept of deep, or geologic, time and its resonances today.

Connections to the land can be fraught, revealing charged histories of ownership, access, and conflict. The South African artist Christine Dixie considers personal history and memory in her intriguing self-portrait *Unravel,* which depicts the artist reflecting on, and seemingly a part of, a magnificent vista of the distant mountains, rolling hills, and lowlands of the Eastern Cape that she calls home (FIG. 99, PLATE 114). The female figure stands outside the frame of the landscape, with her back to the viewer. Her right hand is raised, pulling a thread that leads from the top of the composition to a ball of yarn in her left hand. Her bare feet are set apart and appear ready to take the next step. The title of the work and the figure's pose and gestures are evocative and ambiguous, possibly suggesting the artist's desire to disentangle the history of this landscape and to understand her place within it.

African American artists engage in similar musings in works of art that foreground landscapes or an engagement with nature. Landscapes were the primary subject of the nineteenth-century African American artists Robert S. Duncanson and Edward Mitchell Bannister. Grand views of America's natural beauty were popular themes in mainstream art throughout the nineteenth century. As America expanded across the continent, landscape paintings evoked a sense of the uniqueness of the terrain and the sublime forces of nature, as well as the power and majesty of the new nation. In many ways the visual identity of America as a place was tied to landscape painting. Duncan-

fig. 99 | OPPOSITE

[plate 114]
Christine Dixie
born 1966, South Africa
Unravel
2001
Linocut and etching on paper
154.5 x 94.3 cm
(60 13/16 x 37 1/8 in.)
National Museum of African
Art, Smithsonian Institution,
purchased with funds pro-
vided by the Annie Laurie
Aitken Endowment, 2011-6-4

son and Bannister followed the professional artistic pathways of the day, adhering to standards and trends that were often derived from European models. That these African Americans were able to enter the rarified realm of fine art, despite prevailing notions among white people at the time that black people were inferior by virtue of their race, testifies to their immense talent. (Many of Duncanson's patrons were abolitionists, who demonstrated their political position on slavery in part through supporting Duncanson's efforts.) Duncanson, who was active from the 1850s to the 1870s, worked in the tradition of the Hudson River school painters, who captured the dramatic grandeur of the American landscape along New York's Hudson River and beyond. Duncanson's *Falls of Minnehaha* (FIG. 96, PLATE 115) depicts the majestic falls located in Minneapolis, Minnesota. A major tourist destination in the mid-nineteenth century, the waterfall was evoked in the popular epic poem *The Song of Hiawatha* (1855) by Henry Wadsworth Longfellow. In the poem the young Ojibwa warrior Hiawatha marries Minnehaha, a Dakota maiden whom Longfellow named after the falls. Duncanson depicts a diminutive figure, perhaps Minnehaha, standing on the riverbank, a witness to the beauty of the cascade. Duncanson often chose to couple his romantic landscapes with literary themes, and he brought them together again in *Vale of Kashmir* (SEE FIG. 2, PLATE 6), a painting that was inspired by a poem by the Irishman Thomas Moore and that is also in the Cosby collection.

Longfellow's popular characters Hiawatha and Minnehaha are also the subjects of Mary Edmonia Lewis's 1866 marble sculpture *Marriage of Hiawatha* (PLATE 116). It was a remarkable achievement for Lewis, a woman with Native American (Ojibwa) and African American forebears, to establish herself as a sculptor in a field dominated by white men. She revisited themes related to *The Song of Hiawatha* in many other works during the 1860s and 1870s. As noted above in the discussion of Duncanson's work, visual interpretations of Longfellow's poem were part of a growing fashion in painting, sculpture, and popular representation between the mid-1850s and the 1870s. For Lewis, the subject also reflected her conscious effort to forefront her Native American heritage. While the details of her ancestry remain unclear, she was one of the few artists of color in the nineteenth century to actively construct an identity of difference in both her personal life and her subject matter.[1]

Later in the century, as the literary-landscape tradition began to wane, artists such as Edward Mitchell Bannister followed other popular European-derived styles. Bannister's *Fishing* (PLATE 117) is a genre scene focusing on five young men. The interest in everyday events and people, the informality of the scene, and the loose brushstrokes are typical of the French Barbizon painters, who were drawn to peasant life and picturesque scenes of nature.

African American artists in the late twentieth century approached the genre of landscape as both form and metaphor in a variety of singular modes. Bob Thompson, a 1960s Beat-generation artist, began his short but prolific career at the dawn of the black radical movement in America. Thompson opted out of the political struggles for black power, however, and chose to follow his own aesthetic and cultural instincts. Thompson spent most of his artistic career living in Europe, where he studied the European old masters from the Renaissance to the baroque. His enigmatic paintings have a mythic quality and are often interpretations of the works he encountered in Europe. *Bird with Nudes* (FIGS. 39, 100, PLATE 118) features stylized figures in yellow, red, and gray—expressive rather than natural colors. The narrative is uncertain in this dreamlike image in which threes nudes, a dog, and

fig. 100

[plate 118]
Bob Thompson
1937–1966, United States
Bird with Nudes
1964
Oil on canvas
92 x 122 cm (36 1/4 x 48 in.)
The Collection of Camille O.
and William H. Cosby Jr.

fig. 101

[plate 119]
Hughie Lee-Smith
1915–1999, United States
Festival's End #2 (detail)
1987
Oil on canvas
97.8 x 98.5 cm
(38 1/2 x 38 3/4 in.)
The Collection of Camille O.
and William H. Cosby Jr.

two birds are actors in a strange landscape. Thompson's "colored" people show no racial characteristics, and their unconventional hues serve to dislodge the importance of race as a cultural marker. The artist's curiously misshapen birds, which are a recurring motif in his work, often struggle between independent flight and the grasp of a human hand. The surrealist Hughie Lee-Smith also depicts a moody and almost illegible human narrative within a landscape in *Festival's End #2* (FIG. 101, PLATE 119). The mysterious woman, whose back is turned to the viewer, gazes out over an unfamiliar urban vista. A feeling of melancholy permeates this lonely scene as the streaming fragments of nearby festivities float by. Thompson's and Lee-Smith's non-naturalistic representations present landscapes as imaginative spaces ripe for open-ended interpretations.

A more overtly political approach to the landscape is found in *Roots, Southern Landscape* (FIG. 102, PLATE 121), by the expatriate African American artist Walter Williams. In this dreamy, almost fantastic landscape, children play and butterflies drift around a large, dark, upturned tree root that is entangled in barbed wire. This ominous dead tree seems like an incongruous element in a field full of sunflowers and other colorful foliage. However, upon closer examination, we find that the field of flowers turns into a cotton field. Small figures, perhaps children, pick cotton among several shacks. Williams has fashioned a landscape in which the roots of American slavery and tenant farming are sites of memory wherein the severed roots of the first Africans in America are recalled. However, his depictions of young children, flowers, and butterflies, along with his use of warm, energetic yellow, orange, and pink hues, evoke the promise of renewal.

An interest in design and abstraction is evident in Alma Woodsey Thomas's luminous, brightly hued canvases, which draw on an experience of the natural world rather than just a view of it. An artist of exceptional technical skill, Thomas received extensive formal training in the arts, including a degree in 1924 from Howard University in Washington, D.C., as the art department's first graduate.[2] *A Fantastic Sunset* (PLATE 120) reveals her connections with the Washington Color school but evinces as well the signature style of her late work. Thomas's was a thoroughly modernist aesthetic that combined vibrant colors and static brushstrokes layered into energetic bursts of acrylic paint. In a totally abstract language, Thomas captures the awe-inspiring power and radiance of the sun and expresses something of the joie de vivre of an artist who seems to be at peace with her place in the world.

The artworks in this section show African and African American artists exploring the symbolic structures and affective capacities of the natural world—actual and imagined—and their connections to human experience. Some of these works frame and negotiate personal space and identity; others bear witness to inequities and call out for social justice and environmental stewardship; and still others, finally, accentuate the transcendent, fragile beauty of our world and our moral imperative to safeguard it—and be a part of it—for the benefit of future generations.

NOTES

1. See Buick 2010, chap. 3.

2. Driskell 2001, 41.

fig. 102

[plate 121]
Walter Williams
1920–1998, United States
Roots, Southern Landscape
1978
Oil, sand, enamel, collage
121.3 x 149.3 cm
(47 3/4 x 58 3/4 in.)
The Collection of Camille O.
and William H. Cosby Jr.

plate 111 | OPPOSITE

Papa Ibra Tall
born 1935, Senegal
Tapestry
1964
Cotton, wool, dye
157.5 x 226 cm (62 x 89 in.)
National Museum of African
Art, Smithsonian Institution,
gift of Robert S. McNamara,
84-7-1

plate 112 | RIGHT

Alexander "Skunder"
Boghossian
1937–2003, Ethiopia
Devil Descending
1972
Oil and mixed media on
canvas
152.7 x 122.4 cm
(60 1/8 x 48 3/16 in.)
National Museum of African
Art, Smithsonian Institution,
gift of Basilio F. Ciocci in
memory of Raimondo Ciocci
and Elvira Maone Ciocci,
99-22-1

plate 113

Georgia Papageorge
born 1941, South Africa
*Maasai Steppe Ascending—
Convective Displacement*
1997
Oil stick and graphite on
canvas with volcanic rock
and cloth
239 x 117 cm
(94 1/8 x 46 1/16 in.)
National Museum of African
Art, Smithsonian Institution,
museum purchase, 98-19-1

plate 114

Christine Dixie
born 1966, South Africa
Unravel
2001
Linocut and etching on paper
154.5 x 94.3 cm
(60 13/16 x 37 1/8 in.)
National Museum of African
Art, Smithsonian Institution,
purchased with funds pro-
vided by the Annie Laurie
Aitken Endowment,
2011-6-4

plate 118

Bob Thompson
1937–1966, United States
Bird with Nudes
1964
Oil on canvas
92 x 122 cm (36 1/4 x 48 in.)
The Collection of Camille O.
and William H. Cosby Jr.

plate 107

Crossroads Quilters
Port Gibson, Mississippi
The Ennis Quilt
1997
Collected scrap fabric and
Ennis Cosby's clothing
370.8 x 294.8 cm
(146 x 116 in.)
The Collection of Camille O.
and William H. Cosby Jr.

Nature as Metaphor

N CERTAIN WORKS OF ART in *Conversations,* nature serves as metaphor in exploring intersecting ideas about history, identity, power, knowledge, spirituality, and environmental stewardship. African and African American artistic engagement with the world ranges from naturalism to abstraction to surrealist meditations; these examine in distinctive ways the multifaceted, often flawed relationships that human beings have with one another and with the physical and intellectual environments in which they live.

Selected works of traditional African art demonstrate how artists are keen observers of the natural world and understand the complexities associated

201

with it. Among the Nuna of Burkina Faso, butterflies are harbingers of rain and thus their appearance is closely connected to the start of the farming season. Butterfly masks (PLATE 108) reflect this knowledge as well as the spiritual properties linked with nature, since this and other masks among the Nuna and related groups in the region are representations of nature spirits that combine human and animal form. Both the celestial and the terrestrial domain are suggested in the form of the butterfly mask, which merges the representation of a human head, rendered in high relief, with a huge, bird-like creature, depicted with concentric-circle eyes and a projecting, diamond-shaped bill. Three-dimensional birds and chameleons perch above the massive wings, which are ornamented with red, black, and white geometric motifs, suggesting the patterning of butterfly wings. In this region of Burkina Faso highly entertaining masquerade performances enliven ceremonial and secular occasions. They bring nature spirits into contact with domesticated village life and give humans access to the powerful and protective capacities of the natural world and its denizens.

For the Yoruba of Nigeria, traditional artworks that depict a large bird in the center of a gathering of birds symbolize the control of supernatural forces and the dominance of good over evil (PLATE 109, PLATE 110). The motif designates the power of the herbalist, who is a priest of the gods of healing, Osanyin and Erinle. Birds inhabit the dual realms of sky and earth; as birds take flight, their vantage point provides superior surveillance of the world below. These qualities are positively linked to the exceptional capacities of Yoruba kings and others, such as herbalists, whose leadership skills and specialized knowledge translate into their authority over secular and sacred domains. Through their work such individuals bring order to the world and counterbalance malevolent forces, which can also take flight—particularly at night—and threaten the world of humans.

The natural world serves contemporary African artists, too, as a rich source of

fig. 96 | OVERLEAF, LEFT

[plate 115]
Robert S. Duncanson
1821–1872, United States
Falls of Minnehaha
1862
Oil on canvas
92 x 71.8 cm
(36 1/4 x 28 1/4 in.)
The Collection of Camille O.
and William H. Cosby Jr.

fig. 97 | OVERLEAF, RIGHT

[plate 113]
Georgia Papageorge
born 1941, South Africa
*Maasai Steppe Ascending—
Convective Displacement*
1997
Oil stick and graphite on
canvas with volcanic rock
and cloth
239 x 117 cm
(94 1/8 x 46 1/16 in.)
National Museum of African
Art, Smithsonian Institution,
museum purchase, 98-19-1

fig. 98

[plate 111]
Papa Ibra Tall
born 1935, Senegal
Tapestry
1964
Cotton, wool, dye
157.5 x 226 cm (62 x 89 in.)
National Museum of African
Art, Smithsonian Institution,
gift of Robert S. McNamara,
84-7-1

metaphor. A harmonious world order, for example, is conceived through the intermingling of human and floral imagery in a brightly hued tapestry, from the 1960s, created by the Senegalese modernist Papa Ibra Tall (FIG. 98, PLATE 111). At first it is hard to discern the human forms that emerge and recede amid the highly decorative vegetation that dominates the composition. Then the eyes adjust to the ways that the central figure's head and hands, and the smaller heads to either side, are composed of the surrounding flora—a visualization of intellectual engagement in perfect balance with the natural world.

By contrast, the Ethiopian artist Alexander "Skunder" Boghossian presents a chaotic view of nature, a cosmos out of balance, in *Devil Descending* (PLATE 112). Painted in 1972, the work—along with others produced around that time—captures the instability and tensions leading up to the overthrow of the Ethiopian monarchy in 1974. A fragmented landscape composed of a jumble of geometric forms, graphic symbols, and complex imagery is set against a sky dominated by an orange-red sun, a crescent moon, and a massive predatory creature with shadowy wings outstretched. It is a surreal world clearly threatened by the evil forces set to wreak havoc upon it.

The theme of life out of balance is also explored by the South African artist Georgia Papageorge, who incorporates ground-down volcanic rock from the crater and other areas of Tanzania's Mount Kilimanjaro in *Maasai Steppe Ascending—Convective Displacement* (FIG. 97, PLATE 113). It is one of a series of works in which the artist explores the destructive effects of poor environmental stewardship, with particular emphasis on the decreasing snow cover atop the mountain owing to climate change, deforestation, and charcoal production. A ladder links sky and earth, calling to mind the difficult ascent to the summit or, possibly, the challenging path to transcendence. Papageorge's use of red cloth suggests the bloodlines that bind us to one another, to the geologic sweep of our shared history, and to our mutual obligation to ensure that our world and its natural beauties survive for the benefit of future generations. In this and other works, Papageorge meditates on the concept of deep, or geologic, time and its resonances today.

Connections to the land can be fraught, revealing charged histories of ownership, access, and conflict. The South African artist Christine Dixie considers personal history and memory in her intriguing self-portrait *Unravel,* which depicts the artist reflecting on, and seemingly a part of, a magnificent vista of the distant mountains, rolling hills, and lowlands of the Eastern Cape that she calls home (FIG. 99, PLATE 114). The female figure stands outside the frame of the landscape, with her back to the viewer. Her right hand is raised, pulling a thread that leads from the top of the composition to a ball of yarn in her left hand. Her bare feet are set apart and appear ready to take the next step. The title of the work and the figure's pose and gestures are evocative and ambiguous, possibly suggesting the artist's desire to disentangle the history of this landscape and to understand her place within it.

African American artists engage in similar musings in works of art that foreground landscapes or an engagement with nature. Landscapes were the primary subject of the nineteenth-century African American artists Robert S. Duncanson and Edward Mitchell Bannister. Grand views of America's natural beauty were popular themes in mainstream art throughout the nineteenth century. As America expanded across the continent, landscape paintings evoked a sense of the uniqueness of the terrain and the sublime forces of nature, as well as the power and majesty of the new nation. In many ways the visual identity of America as a place was tied to landscape painting. Duncan-

plate 119

Hughie Lee-Smith
1915–1999, United States
Festival's End #2
1987
Oil on canvas
97.8 x 98.5 cm
(38 1/2 x 38 3/4 in.)
The Collection of Camille O.
and William H. Cosby Jr.

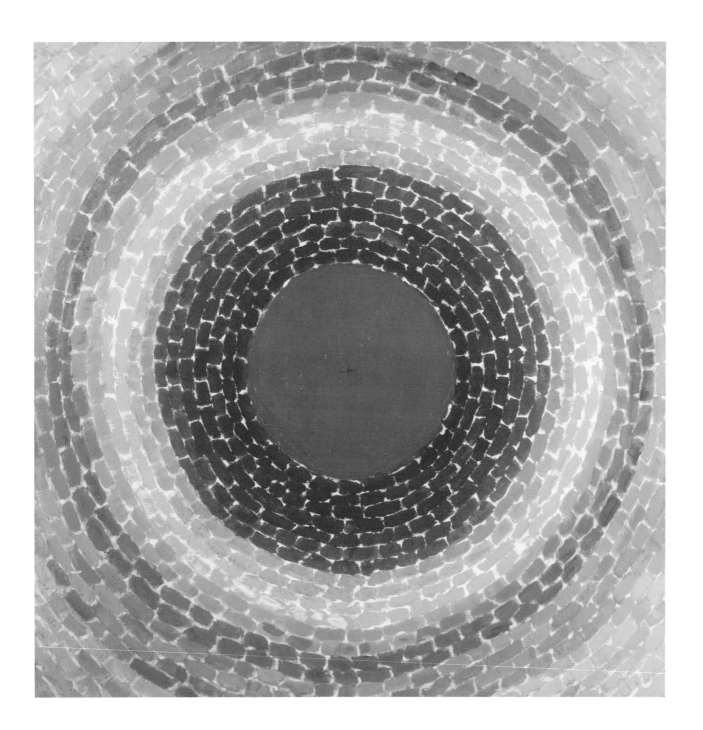

plate 120

Alma Woodsey Thomas
1891–1978, United States
A Fantastic Sunset
1970
Acrylic on canvas
120.8 x 120 cm
(47 1/2 x 47 1/4 in.)
The Collection of Camille O.
and William H. Cosby Jr.

plate 121

Walter Williams
1920–1998, United States
Roots, Southern Landscape
1978
Oil, sand, enamel, collage
121.3 x 149.3 cm
(47 3/4 x 58 3/4 in.)
The Collection of Camille O.
and William H. Cosby Jr.

Music and Urban Culture

USIC SERVES AS INSPIRATION in a number of the African and African American works of art presented in *Conversations*. This theme allows us to examine, without specificity, the degree to which musical forms traveled with enslaved Africans to the Americas, how these forms continued and creatively evolved amid great hardship, how certain African American musical forms reference connections with the continent, and, ultimately, how music was significant in African and African American communities over time.

A selection of traditional African musical instruments serves as a backdrop to this section's broader discussion of music and the urban sphere in contemporary

African and African American arts. Selected artworks address the representation of music making, while others evoke the social settings in which music is experienced and the relationships that unfold there (FIG. 103, PLATE 133). All, however, emphasize the importance of music in forging identity, an identity that is at once highly personal, linked to communities, and globally shared.

Perceptions about Africa invariably include recognition of the continent's long-standing and distinguished musical forms. For those who have traveled or lived in Africa, music seems to be everywhere—blasting out of loudspeakers and car windows, playing on radios or in nightclubs, competing with other forms of entertainment in people's homes, highlighting political rallies, social gatherings, and ceremonial occasions. In these and other contexts, music sets the tone—literally and emotionally—for events that mark the lives of individuals and communities in Africa. This is not to reinforce, however, the unfortunate stereotype that has tended to equate Africa and Africans with music making, particularly drumming, at the expense of recognizing the diversity of the creative endeavors that constitute African expressive culture. Nor is it to suggest that music is constantly playing throughout the day everywhere (or anywhere) in Africa. In a continent as large and varied as Africa there is enormous range in musical forms and the occasions for their playing.

Africa's traditional arts emphasize the importance of music in sculptures depicting musicians (PLATE 122, PLATE 123) and in beautifully made instruments fashioned of wood, ivory, iron, copper alloy, animal skins and hides, gourds, and other materials. In highly decorative examples, human and animal forms are often referenced (PLATE 124, PLATE 125, PLATE 126, PLATE 127). Ownership of such elaborated instruments likely conferred significant status and prestige.

fig. 103 | OVERLEAF, LEFT

[plate 133]
Malick Sidibé
born 1935, Mali
Nuit de Noël (Happy-Club)
1963, printed 2008
Gelatin silver print
Image: 42.5 x 43 cm
(16 3/4 x 16 15/16 in.)
National Museum of African Art, Smithsonian Institution, museum purchase, 2009-12-3

fig. 104 | OVERLEAF, RIGHT

[plate 146]
Romare Bearden
1911–1988, United States
Sitting In at Barron's
1980
Collage on Masonite
100.8 x 75.5 cm
(39 5/8 x 29 3/4 in.)
The Collection of Camille O. and William H. Cosby Jr.

fig. 105

[plate 131]
Luba artist, Kinshasa,
Democratic Republic of
the Congo
Drum
Late 19th to early 20th
century
Wood, reptile skin, pigment
40.3 x 33 x 30.5 cm
(15 7/8 x 13 x 12 in.)
National Museum of African
Art, Smithsonian Institution,
museum purchase, 2013-6-1

An elegant simplicity of form defines a gong made of iron by a Tetela blacksmith, who ornamented it with a few rows of raised designs suggesting body scarification marks (PLATE 128). The human body is also suggested, albeit abstractly, in two Bwa whistles, fashioned with swelling handles that frame the elongated "torsos"; one is wrapped with reptile skin to form decorative linear patterns (PLATE 130). A beautifully carved head with detailed coiffure and earrings tops the gracefully curving neck of a Zande five-string harp, its sound box—or body—covered in animal hide (PLATE 129).

The compact shape and decorative flourishes of a Luba drum suggest a highly abstracted, Janus-faced human head (FIG. 105, PLATE 131). Radiating elliptical patterns heightened in white pigment on both sides of the drum define the eyes and mirror a treatment of the eyes found in Luba and Songye face masks. Protruding vertical panels evoke the nose and ears, and the drumheads are tightly stretched reptile skin. The Asante master sculptor Osei Bonsu also brings together human and animal forms in a drum he carved about 1935 (PLATE 132). The cylindrical body of the drum, with projecting breasts, rests firmly atop a lion, a symbol of leadership and power in Akan culture. Uniting the verbal and the visual, the artist decorated the drum with a range of motifs intended to cue cultural knowledge and proverbs that serve to emphasize, depending on context, the power of the drum society that owns the instrument and the importance of patience and diligence in any endeavor, including music making. The aesthetic power of such expertly fashioned musical instruments is matched with spiritual and intellectual potency by virtue of the culturally specific concepts that inform the linking of human and animal domains.

In distinctive ways, modern and contemporary African works of art reference instruments, music, musicians, and the settings where music is played. A linocut by the Nigerian modernist Solomon Irein Wangboje depicts a seated male figure, possibly in a village setting, playing what appears to be a double-headed drum (PLATE 134). The warm tones and the angle of the musician's head and hands express the energy of drumming performances, which punctuate everyday and ceremonial occasions in towns and villages throughout Africa.

The global urban sphere serves as the setting for works by contemporary African artists that evoke the syncopated rhythms of jazz. Expressive brushstrokes and rich hues, like the lively strains of a jazz riff, play across the canvas of Iba N'Diaye's *Hommage à Bessie Smith* (PLATE 135). Partial views of musicians portrayed in the act of playing complete the energized mood of a jazz club and a global musical form that unites Africa and its diasporas. The African American artist William T. Williams's abstract composition *Perdido* (PLATE 147) also embodies the universal language of music. The title references the composition of the same name, by Juan Tizol, which was performed by many jazz greats, including Duke Ellington, Dizzy Gillespie, and Charlie Parker. Yet another jazz classic is recalled in *Tyilo-Tyilo,* a luminous gouache on paper by the South African artist Louis Maqhubela (FIG. 106, PLATE 136). It celebrates South African township music of the 1960s and recalls the title of the song "Ntyilo-Ntyilo"—*ntyilo-ntyilo* means "little bird," "songbird," or, possibly, "nightingale"—which Miriam Makeba recorded in the 1950s in the Xhosa language and which later became a jazz standard. The lyrics describe someone listening to a beautiful melody, darkened by a voice stating, "There is trouble in the land."[1] The dark square at the center of the painting

fig. 106 | LEFT

[plate 136]
Louis Maqhubela
born 1939, South Africa
Tyilo-Tyilo (detail)
1997
Gouache on paper
74.5 x 56 cm
(29 5/16 x 22 1/16 in.)
National Museum of African
Art, Smithsonian Institution,
museum purchase, 98-19-2

fig. 107 | OPPOSITE

[plate 137]
Wosene Worke Kosrof
born 1950, Ethiopia
The Preacher III (detail)
2000
Acrylic on canvas
111.6 x 92.1 x 3.2 cm
(43 15/16 x 36 1/4 x 1 1/4 in.)
National Museum of African
Art, Smithsonian Institution,
purchased with funds provided by the Annie Laurie
Aitken Endowment, 2001-1-1

might reflect this somber declaration, or it may suggest a night sky filled with brilliant stars, which transforms to become a luminous, sun-filled day.

Wosene Worke Kosrof, who was born in Ethiopia and resides in California, creates works that effectively blend pan-African, Ethiopian, and diasporan themes. The artist is internationally known for his lively, abstract compositions, such as *The Preacher III,* which are energized with an eclectic mix of graphic signs and symbols, including characters from Ethiopia's Amharic and the liturgical language *ge'ez,* that visualize for the artist the rhythms and punctuations of jazz music (FIG. 107, PLATE 137). As a child and young artist growing up in Ethiopia, Wosene—as he prefers to be called—often worked to the accompaniment of music on the radio, which served to introduce him to jazz, which has remained a lifelong passion.[2] The deep red and gold hues of *The Preacher III,* which recall colors prominent in Ethiopian sacred art (SEE FIGS. 54, 63, PLATE 41), evoke that country's long history of Christianity and its links with Byzantine and Coptic histories. The painting demonstrates the ways in which Wosene has investigated through his work his transnational identities and his connections to the multiple places that he calls home—where jazz is ever present.

These bonds to music, particularly jazz as a globally recognized yet quintessentially African American musical form, are forged by African American artists in works that examine issues of race, identity, and place. The story of African Americans in the twentieth century was closely tied to the rise of major cities and the development of urban cultures. The Great Migration of African Americans out of the confines and violence of the Jim Crow South to urban centers such as New York and Chicago affected not only demographics but cultural development as well. The Harlem Renaissance of the 1920s and the Chicago Black Renaissance of the 1930s and 1940s are directly related to the influx of black residents into these urban meccas. Visual artists such as Chicago's Archibald J. Motley Jr. and Harlem's Jacob Lawrence engaged in their artworks the energies derived from the flow of African Americans into urban centers, and in the process created some of the most important representations of African American urban culture in the early twentieth century.

From Chicago to Paris, the flourishing jazz scene of the 1920s and 1930s was a frequent subject for Chicago's master painter of "Negro" life, Archibald J. Motley Jr. A native of New Orleans, Motley followed the currents of the Great Migration to the growing opportunities for blacks in Chicago. Motley was trained at the School of the Art Institute of Chicago, one of the few mainstream institutions that regularly accepted African American artists. The 1927 painting *Stomp* (FIGS. 29, 108, PLATE 141), which captures the frenzy of jazz musicians and "stomping" dancers, is one of the artist's early images of Chicago nightlife. Chicago's South Side was known as one of the centers of blues and the burgeoning jazz scene. *Stomp* is likely the depiction of a so-called black-and-tan club, where a well-heeled clientele, both black and white, freely mingled and enjoyed the new sounds of live jazz entertainment. A somewhat transgressive space, the black-and-tan club often fostered interaction between the races that was considered taboo by both blacks and whites.[3] However, as the art historian Amy Mooney observed, in Motley's hands jazz music seems to have a way of temporarily suspending the racial tensions that structured society at large.[4] His *Bronzeville at Night* (PLATE 142), painted more than twenty years later, returns to Chicago's South Side, to the black entertainment district

fig. 108
[plate 141]
Archibald J. Motley Jr.
1891–1981, United States
Stomp (detail)
1927
Oil on canvas
76.3 x 91.5 cm (30 x 36 in.)
The Collection of Camille O. and William H. Cosby Jr.

fig. 109

[plate 143]
Jacob Lawrence
1917–2000, United States
Blind Musician (detail)
1942
Gouache
53.3 x 73.8 cm (21 x 29 in.)
The Collection of Camille O.
and William H. Cosby Jr.

dubbed Bronzeville. A city street with a massage parlor, a chicken joint, and a liquor store provides an urban framework for Motley's complex view of black identities captured in the comings and goings of an array of African American types.

Jacob Lawrence and Romare Bearden, two of the most acclaimed African American modernists, both engaged the symbiotic relationship of music and black urban cultures, forging new visual languages for modern black identities. The shared experience of music on a city street is the focus of Lawrence's *Blind Musician* (FIGS. 37, 109, PLATE 143). A crowd gathers outside a bar, enraptured by the spectacle of a blind musician playing a guitar with his foot. The musician was perhaps one of the characters Lawrence encountered while working on his Harlem series (1942–43), thirty paintings devoted to everyday life in the neighborhood. Lawrence, with his particular brand of narrative abstraction, tells rich stories of Harlem life in flat, simplified shapes and a limited palette. His *Street Scene, Harlem* (PLATE 144) is a bird's-eye view of the variegated urban environment that includes apartment buildings, hotels, churches, a bar and grill, and more. While the composition is largely structured by the interplay of buildings in an almost abstract pattern, Lawrence includes humanizing details such as stained-glass church windows, clothes hanging from a rooftop clothesline, and children playing jump rope on the street. Like Motley's, Lawrence's teeming urban views reveal the public spaces where black identities are negotiated and shared, a theme that was also explored, though in terms of a more private or personal space, by the mid-twentieth-century expressionist artist Beauford Delaney in his painting *Beauford Delaney's Loft* (FIG. 110, PLATE 145). In the work of Delaney, Lawrence, and Motley, music is a central rallying point for forging relationships both among African Americans and between African Americans and the larger society.

Romare Bearden's aesthetic is often considered a formal manifestation of jazz rhythms. Certainly the seemingly improvisational quality of his collages, the syncopation of elements, and the interaction of tones and colors evoke a jazz sensibility. In addition, Bearden's dedication to the narratives of black music traditions is borne out in his career-spanning interest in the image of the black musician. Bearden synthesized the visual and the audible in his representations of musical culture, which range from southern folk and Delta blues to jazz at Harlem's Savoy Ballroom. *Sitting In at Barron's* (FIG. 104, PLATE 146) is set in Barron's Exclusive Club, a well-known 1920s Harlem nightclub that catered to affluent white people and celebrities both black and white. The piano player in a derby could be a young Duke Ellington or Fats Waller, whose music and theatricality defined the jazz of that era.

The angled perspective of the white-and-black piano keyboard creates a lively visual rhythm in Bearden's collage, one that is also present in the black, white, hatched, and colored blocks in a work on paper entitled *Zongo,* by the Ghanaian artist Atta Kwami (FIG. 111, PLATE 138). Kwami has linked the work to Africa's urban space but not to music making, however. The title—*zongo* is a Hausa term for "settlement" or "encampment"—suggests Ghana's cramped urban neighborhoods largely inhabited by Muslim merchants, while the strips of color echo Ghana's famed strip-woven kente cloth. The rhythms of urban life are captured as well in striking modernist prints by Oluwole Olayemi and Adebisi Fabunmi (PLATE 139, PLATE 140), who form part of Nigeria's Oshogbo movement, which began in the early 1960s and is ongoing.[5] Such comparisons draw the eye to related visual devices of color and pattern that artists employ for distinct purposes in creating expressive, evocative works of art.

As the artworks in this section suggest, African and African American artists explore a range of issues through works that center on the affecting experience of music— the aural, the visual, and the real and imagined human relationships that form around

fig. 110

[plate 145]
Beauford Delaney
1901–1979, United States
Beauford Delaney's Loft
(detail)
1948
Oil on canvas
78.8 x 96.5 cm (31 x 38 in.)
The Collection of Camille O.
and William H. Cosby Jr.

its playing in rural and urban settings. Transcending race, nationality, and culturally specific narratives, the artworks embody music as a universal language.

NOTES

1. For the lyrics, see "Ntyilo-Ntyilo (Bird Song)," South African History Online, accessed February 2014, http://www.sahistory.org.za/archive/ntyilo-ntyilo-bird-song.

2. Kreamer and Purpura 2012, 140.

3. For discussion of black-and-tan clubs, see Mumford 1997, 31–34.

4. Mooney and Motley 2004, 86. For more on Motley, see Powell 2014.

5. From the movement's beginnings, Oshogbo artists have defied categorization; they draw on traditional forms and aesthetic systems in creating modernist works that embrace all media—painting, prints, sculpture, and textiles. For more on the movement and its artists, see Kennedy 1992, 58–86.

fig. 111
[plate 138]
Atta Kwami
born 1956, Ghana
Zongo
2010
Pigment on paper
30.3 x 25.6 cm
(11 15/16 x 10 1/16 in.)
National Museum of African
Art, Smithsonian Institution,
gift of the artist in honor of
Philip L. Ravenhill, 2010-11-1

plate 122 | FAR LEFT

Yoruba artist, Nigeria
Staff
Mid-20th century
Wood, indigo
41.5 x 8.7 x 21.7 cm
(16 5/16 x 3 7/16 x 8 9/16 in.)
National Museum of African
Art, Smithsonian Institution,
gift of Walt Disney World
Co., a subsidiary of The Walt
Disney Company, 2005-6-354

plate 123 | LEFT

Mbala artist, Democratic
Republic of the Congo
Male figure
Late 19th to early 20th
century
Wood
29.8 x 41.6 x 15.9 cm
(11 3/4 x 16 3/8 x 6 1/4 in.)
National Museum of African
Art, Smithsonian Institution,
gift of Walt Disney World
Co., a subsidiary of The Walt
Disney Company, 2005-6-186

plate 128 | RIGHT

Tetela artist or Nkutshu
artist, Democratic Republic
of the Congo
Gong
19th to 20th century
Iron
53.3 x 24.8 x 11 cm
(21 x 9 3/4 x 4 5/16 in.)
National Museum of African
Art, Smithsonian Institution,
gift of Tom Joyce and mu-
seum purchase with funds
donated by Carl Jennings,
2002-10-23

plate 129 | FAR RIGHT

Zande artist, Democratic
Republic of the Congo
Harp
Early 20th century
Wood, hide, metal
90.2 x 22.9 cm
(35 1/2 x 9 in.)
National Museum of African
Art, Smithsonian Institution,
museum purchase, 85-17-1

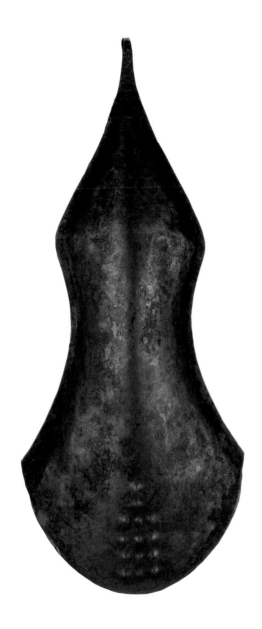

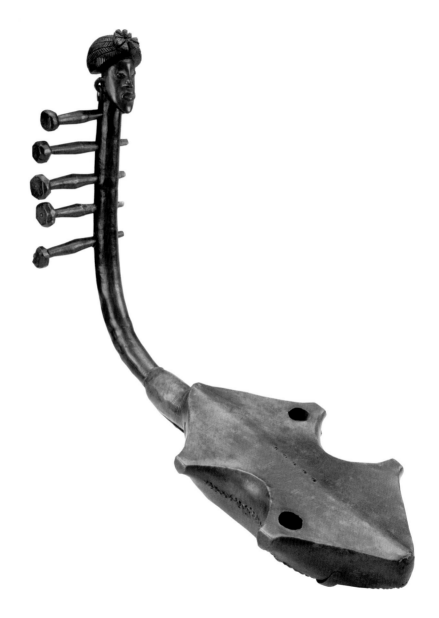

plate 130 | LEFT TO RIGHT

Bwa artist, Burkina Faso
Whistle
Mid-20th century
Wood
26.7 x 7.6 x 3.2 cm
(10 1/2 x 3 x 1 1/4 in.)
National Museum of African
Art, Smithsonian Institution,
gift of Saul Bellow, 78-43-2

Bwa artist, Burkina Faso
Whistle
Mid-20th century
Wood, reptile skin
26.7 x 7.6 x 3.2 cm
(10 1/2 x 3 x 1 1/4 in.)
National Museum of African
Art, Smithsonian Institution,
gift of Warren M. Robbins,
83-13-5

Luba artist, Kinshasa,
Democratic Republic of
the Congo
Drum
Late 19th to early 20th
century
Wood, reptile skin, pigment
40.3 x 33 x 30.5 cm
(15 7/8 x 13 x 12 in.)
National Museum of African
Art, Smithsonian Institution,
museum purchase, 2013-6-1

plate 132

Osei Bonsu
1900–1977, Asante
artist, Ghana
Drum
c. 1935
Wood, hide, paint, metal
102.9 x 38.1 x 48.9 cm
(40 1/2 x 15 x 19 1/4 in.)
National Museum of African
Art, Smithsonian Institution,
gift of Dr. Robert Portman,
81-20-1

Malick Sidibé
born 1935, Mali
Nuit de Noël (Happy-Club)
1963, printed 2008
Gelatin silver print
Image: 42.5 x 43 cm
(16 3/4 x 16 15/16 in.)
Sheet: 61 x 50 cm
(24 x 19 11/16 in.)
National Museum of African
Art, Smithsonian Institution,
museum purchase, 2009-12-3

Linocut 2/12   The Music Maker — Mood V   Irein Wangboje 1965.

plate 134 | LEFT

Solomon Irein Wangboje
1930–1998, Nigeria
The Music Maker—Mood V
1965
Linocut on paper
36.2 x 29.8 cm
(14 1/4 x 11 3/4 in.)
National Museum of African
Art, Smithsonian Institution,
gift of Amb. and Mrs. Ben-
jamin Hill Brown Jr., 76-3-18

plate 135 | OPPOSITE

Iba N'Diaye
1928–2008, Senegal
Hommage à Bessie Smith
1987
Oil on canvas
300.4 x 905 cm
(118 1/4 x 356 5/16 in.)
National Museum of African
Art, Smithsonian Institution,
gift of Mme Diouf and mu-
seum purchase, 2002-13-1

plate 136

Louis Maqhubela
born 1939, South Africa
Tyilo-Tyilo
1997
Gouache on paper
74.5 x 56 cm
(29 5/16 x 22 1/16 in.)
National Museum of African
Art, Smithsonian Institution,
museum purchase, 98-19-2

plate 137

Wosene Worke Kosrof
born 1950, Ethiopia
The Preacher III
2000
Acrylic on canvas
111.6 x 92.1 x 3.2 cm
(43 15/16 x 36 1/4 x 1 1/4 in.)
National Museum of African
Art, Smithsonian Institution,
purchased with funds pro-
vided by the Annie Laurie
Aitken Endowment, 2001-1-1

S.P.   ZONGO   ATTA KWAMI 2010

plate 138

Atta Kwami
born 1956, Ghana
Zongo
2010
Pigment on paper
30.3 x 25.6 cm
(11 15/16 x 10 1/16 in.)
National Museum of African
Art, Smithsonian Institution,
gift of the artist in honor of
Philip L. Ravenhill, 2010-11-1

plate 139 | RIGHT, TOP

Oluwole Olayemi
born 1947, Nigeria
Tinubu Square Lagos
1970
Black ink on white paper
30.5 x 45.7 cm (12 x 18 in.)
National Museum of African
Art, Smithsonian Institution,
gift of the Wil and Irene Petty
Collection, 2008-5-32

plate 140 | RIGHT, BOTTOM

Adebisi Fabunmi
born 1945, Ghana
Benin City
1970
Linocut
56.6 x 69.4 cm
(22 5/16 x 27 5/16 in.)
National Museum of African
Art, Smithsonian Institution,
gift of the Wil and Irene Petty
Collection, 2008-5-19

plate 143 | LEFT

Jacob Lawrence
1917–2000, United States
Blind Musician
1942
Gouache
53.3 x 73.8 cm (21 x 29 in.)
The Collection of Camille O.
and William H. Cosby Jr.

plate 144 | OPPOSITE

Jacob Lawrence
1917–2000, United States
Street Scene, Harlem
1942
Gouache on board
55.3 x 75.5 cm
(21 3/4 x 29 3/4 in.)
The Collection of Camille O.
and William H. Cosby Jr.

plate 145 | OPPOSITE

Beauford Delaney
1901–1979, United States
Beauford Delaney's Loft
1948
Oil on canvas
78.8 x 96.5 cm (31 x 38 in.)
The Collection of Camille O.
and William H. Cosby Jr.

plate 146 | RIGHT

Romare Bearden
1911–1988, United States
Sitting In at Barron's
1980
Collage on Masonite
100.8 x 75.5 cm
(39 5/8 x 29 3/4 in.)
The Collection of Camille O.
and William H. Cosby Jr.

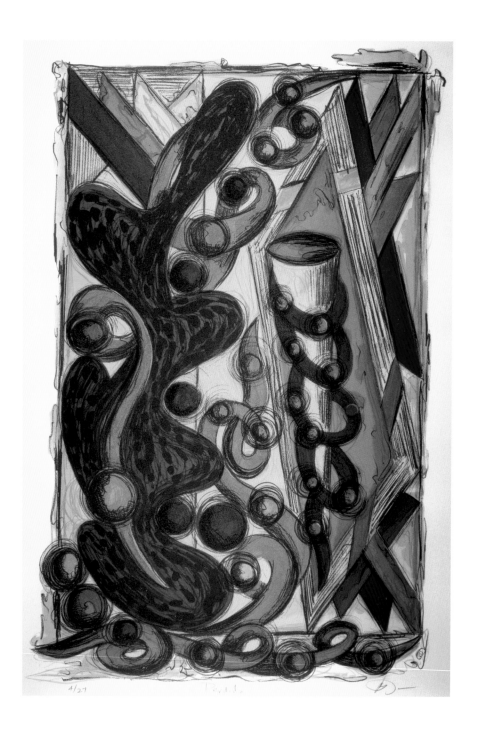

plate 147

William T. Williams
born 1942, United States
Perdido
1991
Lithograph
104.3 x 73.8 cm (41 x 29 in.)
The Collection of Camille O.
and William H. Cosby Jr.

Selected Bibliography

Arens, W., and Ivan Karp, eds. 1989. *Creativity of Power: Cosmology and Action in African Societies.* Washington, D.C.: Smithsonian Institution Press.

Ater, Renée. 2011. *Remaking Race and History: The Sculpture of Meta Warrick Fuller.* Berkeley: University of California Press.

Barnwell, Andrea D. [Andrea Barnwell Brownlee]. 2002. *Charles White.* The David C. Driskell Series of African American Art 1. San Francisco: Pomegranate.

Binkley, David, Bryna Freyer, Christine Mullen Kreamer, Andrea Nicolls, and Allyson Purpura. 2011. "Building a National Collection of African Art: The Life History of a Museum." In *Representing Africa in American Art Museums: A Century of Collecting and Display,* edited by Kathleen Bickford Berzock and Christa Clarke, 265–88. Seattle: University of Washington Press.

Buick, Kirsten Pai. 2010. *Child of the Fire: Mary Edmonia Lewis and the Problem of Art History's Black and Indian Subject.* Durham, N.C.: Duke University Press.

Childs, Adrienne L. 2009. *Margo Humphrey.* The David C. Driskell Series of African American Art 7. Petaluma, Calif.: Pomegranate Communications.

———. 2012. "Tanner and 'Oriental' Africa." In *Henry Ossawa Tanner: Modern Spirit,* edited by Anna O. Marley, 98–105. Philadelphia: Pennsylvania Academy of the Fine Arts.

Comaroff, Jean, and John Comaroff. 1991. *Of Revelation and Revolution.* Vol. 1, *Christianity, Colonialism and Consciousness in South Africa.* Chicago: University of Chicago Press.

Drewal, Henry John. 2008. *Mami Wata: Arts for Water Spirits in Africa and Its Diasporas.* Los Angeles: Fowler Museum at UCLA.

Driskell, David C. 1976. *Two Centuries of Black American Art.* Los Angeles: Los Angeles County Museum of Art.

――――. 2001. *The Other Side of Color: African American Art in the Collection of Camille O. and William H. Cosby Jr.* San Francisco: Pomegranate.

Heldman, Marilyn. 1993. "Maryam Seyon: Mary of Zion." In *African Zion: The Sacred Art of Ethiopia,* 71–100. Catalogue by Marilyn Heldman with Stuart C. Munro-Hay. New Haven: Yale University Press; Fort Worth: InterCultura; Baltimore: The Walters Art Gallery; Addis Ababa: The Institute of Ethiopian Studies.

Holdstock, T. Len. 2000. *Re-examining Psychology: Critical Perspectives and African Insights.* London: Routledge.

Hughes, Langston. 1995. *The Collected Poems of Langston Hughes.* Edited by Arnold Rampersad and David Roessel. New York: Vintage.

Jackson, Michael, and Ivan Karp, eds. 1990. *Personhood and Agency: The Experience of Self and Other in African Cultures; Papers Presented at a Symposium on African Folk Models and Their Application, Held at Uppsala University, August 23–30, 1987.* Uppsala: Uppsala University.

Johnson, James Weldon. 1927. *God's Trombones: Seven Negro Sermons in Verse.* New York: Viking Press.

Kaphagawani, Didier N. 1998. "African Conceptions of Personhood and Intellectual Identities." In *The African Philosophy Reader,* edited by P. H. Coetzee and A. P. J. Roux, 169–76. London: Routledge.

Kennedy, Jean. 1992. *New Currents, Ancient Rivers: Contemporary African Artists in a Generation of Change.* Washington, D.C.; London: Smithsonian Institution Press.

Kreamer, Christine Mullen. 2007. "Circumscribing Space." In *Inscribing Meaning: Writing and Graphic Systems in African Art,* by Christine Mullen Kreamer, Mary Nooter Roberts, Elizabeth Harney, and Allyson Purpura, 159–75. Washington, D.C.: Smithsonian National Museum of African Art; Milan: 5 Continents Press.

Kreamer, Christine Mullen, and Allyson Purpura. 2012. "Visual Poetry, Performing Script: The Art of Wosene Worke Kosrof." *Nka* 31 (Fall): 139–54.

McGee, Julie L. 2011. "Offerings from the Studio, Heart, and Mind: David C. Driskell in Conversation with Julie L. McGee." In *Creative Spirit: The Art of David C. Driskell,* 24–88. College Park, Md.: David C. Driskell Center at the University of Maryland.

Milbourne, Karen E. 2013. *Earth Matters: Land as Material and Metaphor in the Arts of Africa.* Washington, D.C.: Smithsonian National Museum of African Art; New York: Monacelli Press.

Mooney, Amy M., and Archibald John Motley. 2004. *Archibald J. Motley Jr.* The David C. Driskell Series of African American Art 4. San Francisco: Pomegranate.

Mumford, Kevin J. 1997. *Interzones: Black/White Sex Districts in Chicago and New York in the Early Twentieth Century.* New York: Columbia University Press.

Powell, Richard J. 2012. "Tanner and Transcendence." In *Henry Ossawa Tanner: Modern Spirit,* edited by Anna O. Marley, 56–65. Philadelphia: Pennsylvania Academy of the Fine Arts.

――――, ed. 2014. *Archibald Motley: Jazz Age Modernist.* Durham, N.C.: Nasher Museum of Art at Duke University; Durham: Duke University Press.

Powell, Richard J. et al. 2006. *Conjuring Bearden.* Durham, N.C.: Nasher Museum of Art at Duke University; Durham: Duke University Press.

Roberts, John W. 1999. "Horace Pippin and the African American Vernacular." *Cultural Critique* 41: 5–36.

Simmel, Georg. 1950. *The Sociology of Georg Simmel.* Translated and edited by Kurt H. Wolff. Glencoe, Ill.: Free Press.

Skunder Boghossian: Artist from Ethiopia; Paintings of Portraits and Ways of Life in His African Homeland. 1962. New York: Merton D. Simpson Gallery.

Thompson, Barbara. 2008. "The African Female Body in the Cultural Imagination." In *Black Womanhood: Images, Icons, and Ideologies of the African Body,* edited by Barbara Thompson, 27–47. Hanover, N.H.: Hood Museum of Art, Dartmouth College; Seattle: University of Washington Press.

Thompson, Robert Farris. 1984. *Flash of the Spirit: African and Afro-American Art and Philosophy.* New York: Vintage.

Van Wyk, Gary. 2013. "Art Practice in Tanzania: Landscape, Soundscape, Endurance." In *Shangaa: Art of Tanzania,* edited by Gary Van Wyk, 53–83. New York: Queensborough Community College, The City University College of New York.

Weber, Max. 1964. *The Theory of Social and Economic Organization.* Translated by A. M. Henderson and Talcott Parsons. New York: Free Press.

Williamson, Sue. 2009. *South African Art Now.* New York: Collins Design.

Williamson, Sue, and Ashraf Jamal. 1996. "David Koloane: Darkness Visible." In *Art in South Africa: The Future Present,* 56–57. Cape Town: David Philip.

Willis, Deborah, ed. 2010. *Black Venus 2010: They Called Her "Hottentot."* Philadelphia: Temple University Press.

Index

Page numbers in **bold** type indicate figures.

255